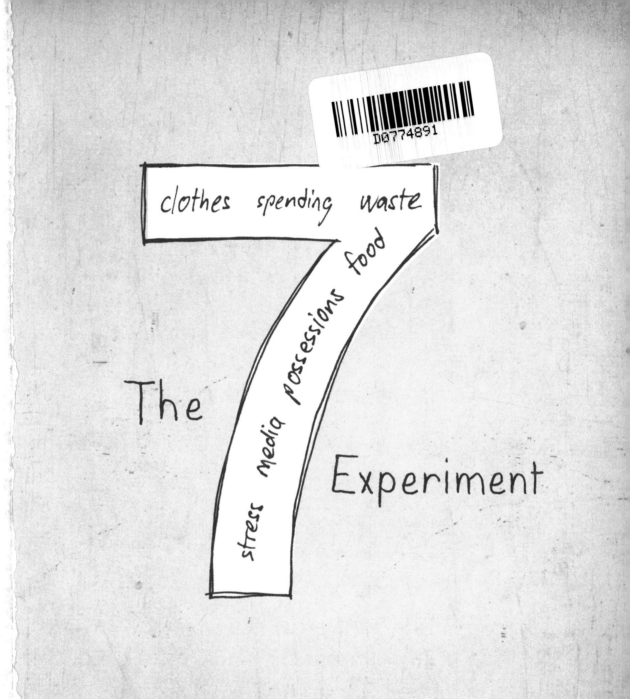

clothes spending waste

food

possessions

media

stress

The

7

Experiment

staging your own mutiny against excess

Jen Hatmaker

LifeWay Press®
Nashville, Tennessee

The 7 Hatmakers: Brandon + Jen with Gavin, Sydney, Caleb, Ben, + Remy

Published by LifeWay Press®
© 2012 Jen Hatmaker
Reprinted 2016

This resource is based on the book 7: An Experimental Mutiny against Excess ©2012 by Jen Hatmaker.
Published in association with the literary agency of Alive Communications, Inc., 7680 Goddard Street, Suite
200, Colorado Springs, CO 80920, www.alivecommunications.com.

ISBN 978-1-4158-7418-9
Item 005515741

Dewey decimal classification: 178
Subject headings: GREED \ MATERIALISM \ LIFESTYLES

Unless otherwise noted, all Scripture quotations are taken from the Holman Christian Standard Bible®,
Copyright © 1999, 2000, 2002, 2003, 2009 by Holman Bible Publishers. Used by permission. Holman
Christian Standard Bible®, Holman CSB®, and HCSB® are federally registered trademarks of Holman Bible
Publishers. Scripture quotations marked NIV are from the Holy Bible, New International Version, copyright
© 1973, 1978, 1984 by International Bible Society. Scripture quotations marked NASB are from the New
American Standard Bible®, Copyright © 1960, 1962, 1963, 1968, 1971, 1972, 1973, 1975, 1977, 1995 by The
Lockman Foundation. Used by permission. (www.lockman.org). Scriptures marked NKJV are from the New
King James Version. Copyright © 1979, 1980, 1982, Thomas Nelson, Inc., Publishers.

To order additional copies of this resource, write to LifeWay Church Resources Customer Service; One
LifeWay Plaza; Nashville, TN 37234-0113; fax 615.251.5933; phone 800.458.2772; email orderentry@lifeway.
com; order online at www.lifeway.com; or visit the LifeWay Christian Store serving you.

Printed in the United States of America

Adult Ministry Publishing
LifeWay Church Resources
One LifeWay Plaza
Nashville, TN 37234-0152

Contents

Week 1
INTRO
7

Week 2
FOOD
27

Week 3
CLOTHING
47

Week 4
POSSESSIONS
67

Week 5
MEDIA
87

Week 6
WASTE
107

Week 7
SPENDING
127

Week 8
STRESS
147

Week 9
WRAP UP
167

Jen Hatmaker and her family live in Austin, Texas, where the city motto is "Keep Austin Weird," and they work hard to do their part. Jen's eight previous books include *Interrupted* and *A Modern Girl's Guide to Bible Study*. She and her husband, Brandon, planted Austin New Church in an economically and ethnically diverse, socially unique, urban area of the city in 2008. They are in the greatest adventure of their lives and have made some incredible new partnerships in ministry. They've seen their world turned upside down as they've considered what it means to ask God how to live and not just what to do. But it's a good upside down, as part of that discovery has included adopting two children from Ethiopia who joined the three they already had. Together they all keep Austin weird and seek to glorify God as they do.

Encouragement Before You Begin The 7 Experiment

Here you are holding *The 7 Experiment* Bible study, and let me be the first to tell you: do not be afraid. My book 7—the journey in which my family, friends, and I embarked on seven fasts from seven areas of excess in seven months—has lived out in the world for a year, and if I had a nickel for every time someone said, "Just downloaded 7. Petrified …" I'd have, well, a lot of nickels.

People have copped to buying 7 and hiding it under their bed, pretending it didn't exist and disavowing their choice to purchase it in the first place. *The 7 Experiment* is not about guilt or condemnation or creating some template to fit us all or pointing a finger. This is about liberation. Trust me, with me as your guide, there is not possibly room for sanctimonious posturing. You've got yourself a good old-fashioned anomaly on your hands with me as someone who chose to speak from the middle of the pack—undeveloped, unfinished, undone myself. I find this material as challenging as you do.

But I also have the benefit of hindsight, having already completed a longer version of *The 7 Experiment,* and let me tell you: These are the opening notes of a good song. In fact, at the end of each week, I included the conclusion I wrote in my original 7 experiment for each area of excess, because I wanted you to read the raw, unedited emotions 7 produced in me. (I've also instructed my editors to leave a journaling page at the end of each week for you to do the same.) If we are willing to offer these blind spots—indulgence, extravagance, greed, excess—to Jesus, we can believe Him for freedom on the other side. There is a bigger story to live, and God is drawing us into it. It is thrilling and good and radical; the gospel life has no equal.

So, welcome. May I humbly take your hand and walk with you for the next few weeks? Do not be afraid of what God may ask of you, because His will always furthers the kingdom, and there is nothing better to spend our last breath on; this is living. We can trust Scripture and Jesus' example and God's truth. His mercies are new every morning. Great is His faithfulness.

Jen

*I've been influenced by the incredible kingdom work of many different authors and organizations, but the mention of them in *The 7 Experiment* should not be construed as an endorsement of all that the mentioned authors and organizations say and do.

Group Suggestions

I have a personality that would land me in prison without wise intervention, but I married Mr. Responsible who has rescued me from disaster more than I'd like to admit. So *The 7 Experiment* sounds straightforward to you, but to me, it sounded like an opportunity to hedge. I've polished up the phrase "extenuating circumstance." I clearly need help to keep me on the straight and narrow.

Enter The Council: Six friends, six personalities, six chances to keep 7 from derailing. The seven of us conferred on all things 7. They were advisors, cheerleaders, decision-makers, counselors, collaborators, and brainstormers. They were not only my personal think tank but participants. I can't imagine 7 without them. Likely, you are launching *The 7 Experiment* with a small group too, maybe through your church, book club, friend circle, or family.

First, bravo. I applaud you tackling this challenging material. I wish I were a fly on the wall as you study Scripture and stage your own mutinies against excess.

Second, I hope you'll set the right tone with your group: mercy, grace, honesty, humility, and a fierce commitment to resist the shackles of guilt. Create safe places to flesh these ideas out without fear of comparison. We're all just doing our best, leaning into our mission and searching the will of God. I wrote from a place of repentance, not arrogance. I included my own personal failures and bad attitudes. I'm so not here to boss you around or make you feel guilty.

Third, your group will have many options to tackle excess each week. There is no formula. There are many means to a similar end. This should create rich discussion and interesting viewpoints. *The 7 Experiment* is primarily a spiritual exercise, so help one another battle our human tendencies toward legalism.

Finally, let me dispel the notion that you need to have these areas licked to facilitate or participate in a group. I started 7 from ground zero. All that is required is a desire to learn and a willing heart. When your group meets, allow the Holy Spirit to guide your time together. Talk about what God has taught you from the previous week's fast. Then watch the video teaching session and discuss the questions provided to help you launch into the next week's fast.

I am diligently praying for you. May God lead us into the gospel in any way, every way. Let's pray together one simple request: Jesus, may there be more of You and Your kingdom and less of us and our junk. Your kingdom come, Your will be done on earth as it is in heaven.

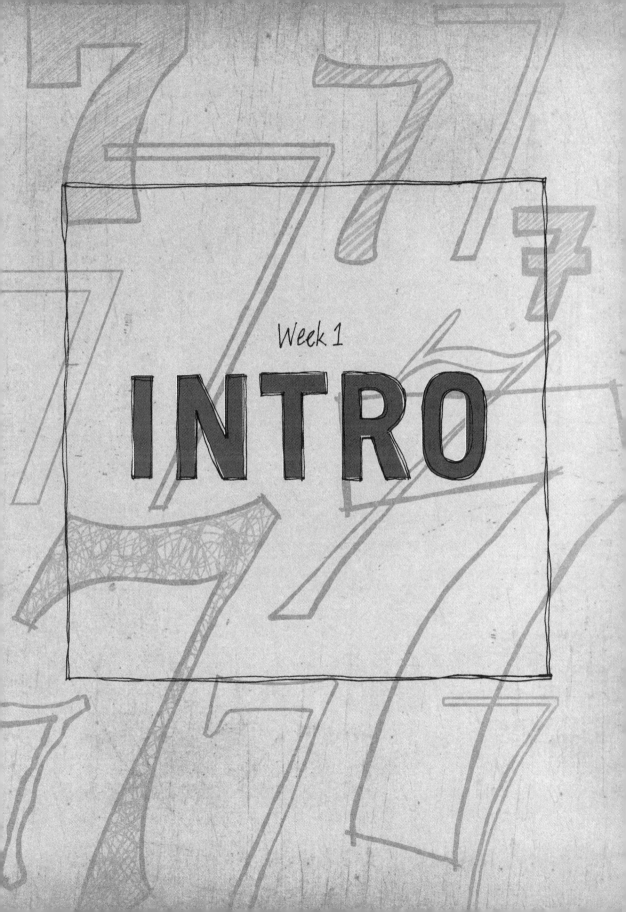

Week 1

INTRO

Video Notes

Group Guide

If your group doesn't know each other, introduce yourself and share what you hope to gain from The 7 Experiment.

How has excess in your life distracted you from God's kingdom work?

Have you ever fasted before? If so, describe the circumstances. If not, what do you anticipate as you fast from excess during The 7 Experiment?

How do you feel about pursuing "less of me, more of God"?

As you begin The 7 Experiment, what do you think God wants to do with your life? What do you think He's calling you to give up? Where do you think He's calling you to serve?

Video session downloads available at www.lifeway.com/jenhatmaker

Getting Ready

We recently adopted two Ethiopian darlings; Ben, 8, and Remy, 6. They've been in America about eight months. Until then, they lived hard stories in hard places. No easy path lands you in the adoption pipeline in a developing country. When we picked them up, they had everything they owned in a tiny bag: the picture albums and a couple of toys we sent them, and the clothes on their backs. That's it. They'd known hunger. They'd known poverty. They'd known desperation. People, they'd slept on the streets.

Ben let out a monstrous, dramatic sigh the other day, like he was contemplating how hard life was, shaking his head, raging against the system. Expecting a genuine difficulty or perhaps a hard memory he was working through, I said: "Ben? What's wrong, honey?"

Big sigh, throwing his hands in the air.

"Mom? WHY CAN'T I JUST HAVE A HORSE?!"

Of course, I burst out laughing and he fled to his room, disgruntled and persecuted because we won't put a horse in our teeny suburban backyard. My, my. How American entitlement has quickly rubbed off on him. His new First-World problems abound apparently.

But before I leave my son under the bus, let me confess a small fraction of the thoughts I've entertained.

> *Why can't I just have* a newer car for once in my life?

> *Why can't I just have* cuter clothes and more of them?

> *Why can't I just have* nice pots and pans instead of these wretched, scratched ones?

> *Why can't I just have* fluffy towels like at Hill Country Hyatt?

> *Why can't I just have* a house with two more rooms? And a jet bathtub?

> *Why can't I just have* a few fancy vacations? Like to Italy or something?

Good reader, what have you wished you could "just have" lately?

Jesus talked repeatedly about people with privileges, riches, advantages. He was always saying how rich people were favored and that our luxuries were granted to us on merit. *Enjoy them, rich folks! It's all for you, and you're awesome!* OPPOSITE DAY! Just kidding. I can't find a single word Jesus spoke that bodes well for rich people at the top of the food chain.

"Woe to you who are rich, for you have received your comfort." Luke 6:24

"As for the seed that fell among thorns, these are the ones who, when they have heard, go on their way and are choked with worries, riches, and pleasures of life, and produce no mature fruit." Luke 8:14

"The Parable of the Rich Fool." Nice title, and here is the punch line:

"That's how it is with the one who stores up treasure for himself and is not rich toward God." Luke 12:21

"He has satisfied the hungry with good things and sent the rich away empty." Luke 1:53

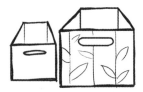

Read Matthew 19:16–22.

Luke 18:18 further tells us this young man was a ruler, so not only does he have money, but he has power and position. In Matthew 19:16 he asked, "What good must I do to have eternal life?"

What does the young man's question to Jesus tell you?

Why on earth, of all the ways Jesus could've challenged him, do you think He answered like He did in Matthew 19:21?

Then, naturally, we get this gem in verse 23, in which I feel deeply connected to Jesus for His use of outrageous hyperbole. (Exaggeration is my medium.) Jesus is seriously making a point by painting the picture of shoving a camel—weighing roughly 2,000 pounds—through the eye of a needle—measuring about half a millimeter. Lest anyone manipulate a lesser metaphor, like fitting a tall guy through a small gate or cramming your foot into a shoe one size too small, Jesus crafts this impossible scenario no listener could minimize.

Rich people able to receive Jesus' kingdom …

It's that hard.

This little story was no problem for me most of my life. I mean, bummer for all those rich people! Whew! What a mess they are. Jesus is not playing. Like the T-shirt I wore in high school said, y'all better "get right … or get left!" (I'm sorry, Everyone Who Knew Me Then.)

Then things started getting weird for me. Rogue thoughts about my own wealth began infiltrating my brain, where I'd cleared space for more comfortable ideas, like, for instance, how to have a happy life. These intruders started questioning the (fat, slothful, apathetic) residents in my mind, asking about the rest of the world and how are you spending your money and why do you have bins of stuff in every corner of your house and do you have a responsibility to those who suffer and does the way you spend your money matter?

You can see why I hated these new tenants.

What have the residents in your brain always told you about what you own? It's OK to be honest.

Do you have any intruders? If so, what are they asking?

Rich White Dudes

Then the intruders, aided and abetted by Jesus, staged a mutiny. The catalyst was the week we housed 12 evacuees from Hurricane Ike. (Our little church, four months old at the time, took in 80 strangers from the coast that had nowhere to go.) We'd moved our three kids into our bedroom, washed sheets, blown up mattresses, rolled out sleeping bags, and readied the house for an onslaught. As carloads arrived and we welcomed them in, one 10-year-old boy walked in our home, looked around with huge eyes, and hollered:

"Dad! This white dude is RICH!"

For years I didn't realize this, because so many others had more. We were surrounded by extreme affluence, which tricks you into thinking you're in the middle of the pack. I mean, sure, we have 2,400 square feet for only five humans to live in, but we haven't traveled to Ireland and my kids are in public school, so how rich could we be? (Roll eyes here.)

But it gets fuzzy once you spend time with people below your rung. I started seeing my stuff with fresh eyes, realizing we had everything. I mean *everything*. We've never missed a meal or even skimped on one. We have a beautiful home in a great neighborhood. Our kids are in an exemplary Texas school. We drive two cars under warranty. We've never gone a day without health insurance. Our closets are overflowing. We throw away food we didn't eat, clothes we barely wore, trash that will never disintegrate, stuff that fell out of fashion.

And I was so blinded, I didn't even know we were rich.

How can we be socially responsible if unaware that we reside in the top percentage of wealth in the world? (You probably do too: Make $35,000 a year? Top 4 percent. $50,000? Top 1 percent.[1]) Excess has impaired perspective in America; we are the richest people on earth, praying to get richer. We're tangled in unmanageable debt while feeding the machine, because we feel entitled to more. What does it communicate when *half the global population lives on less than $2 a day*, and we can't manage a fulfilling life on $25,000 (almost 35 times that amount)? $50,000 (almost 70 times that amount)?[2] It says we have too much and it is ruining us.

It was certainly ruining me. The day I am unaware of my privileges and unmoved by my greed is the day something has to change. I couldn't escape the excess or see beyond my comforts though. I wrung my hands and commiserated with Brandon but couldn't fathom an avenue out. We'd done some first-tier reductions, freeing up excess to share, but still … the white dude was really rich.

Have you ever considered yourself rich? Does your response come from comparing yourself to others? And if so, do you compare yourself to folks above your rung or below it? Why?

I totally identify with the rich young ruler when "he went away grieving, because he had many possessions" (Matt. 19:22).

How do you feel after reading the last few paragraphs? How does a challenge against our American luxuries make you feel?

It's interesting that Jesus gently discarded all this young man's good behaviors and instead plowed into a systemic issue separating him from the kingdom of God: wealth and position. Rather than affirming the lovely side dishes, He went straight to the meat of the matter and totally shocked this well-behaved young man, *who was doing so much right*. I mean, we could understand a rebuttal for a wife-beater or a child abuser or a swindler, but this guy diligently kept the commandments and even wanted to know what else he could do.

He was trying hard, flying right, on the up and up.

Then Jesus told him, "It's not about what you're doing right; it's about what you cherish."

We can figure out what we cherish by how we feel when it is threatened.

How would you feel if God asked you to part ways with your stuff? (Make it real: your house, your neighborhood, your cars, your comforts.)

If you're a believer, how does it feel to have your good behavior discredited compared to how you've handled money and possessions?

For the longest time, I made peace with this story by interpreting it as an exception. In other words, Jesus said this because He knew something sinister about this kid. He must have been embarrassingly greedy, or maybe he was oppressing his people. Whatever it was, this is way too dramatic to apply to normal folks like me. Jesus was handling this particular rich young ruler, and this was *his* issue.

But a higher view of Jesus' teachings shows me something different. I see a theme, a ubiquitous issue, a recurring condition that hinders the kingdom and stops potential Christ-followers short of actually following Christ.

Wealth.

I believe Jesus is telling us something that actually might apply to all of us. I think there really is a problem, and if Jesus is serious, then far more than fearing poverty or discomfort, we should worry about our prosperity. It is the kryptonite of true discipleship, according to Jesus.

Which is the worst news ever for American Christians.

Read Matthew 19:23-25. I find the disciples' reaction telling. Why do you think they were "utterly astonished" after Jesus' statement? What was so shocking?

The disciples watched Jesus engage tax collectors (notorious sharks), thieves, prostitutes, liars, government oppressors, religious oppressors, Gentile outsiders, adulterers. He feared no confrontation, no matter how dangerous or nefarious. He never held His tongue—until the appointed day of His death, when His silence to His accusers hastened the cross, rescuing humanity and splitting history in two. If there was something to call out, Jesus called it out.

No problem.

We're good with Jesus reprimanding adultery and tomfoolery and extortion and self-righteousness. Right on, JC! Let 'em have it! This nonsense has gone on long enough, we say! This is a civilized society, and we can't be having all this mess. You people quit stealing and lying and messing around with your neighbor's husband and drinking bathtub gin. And when Jesus gives you a good old-fashioned what-for, we'll stand over here and nod our heads like, "Mmm-hmm. Sad. I really hope she gets better about this."

Those reprimands don't shock any of us.

But this one does.

Rich people misbehaving? Yes. Rich people behaving well? This is confusing. We, too, are greatly astonished that Jesus thinks this fella is in serious trouble. And Jesus didn't even chase him down, explaining things better or giving him a plan for breaking up with his wealth or stepping down gradually. Jesus just let him go, walking away rich and miserable, wanting the kingdom but unwilling to go this far for it.

List everything you can think of, even beyond the churchy answers, as to why Jesus sets wealth and position up as enemies of the gospel, nearly impossible to reconcile ... even for good people.

So let's just stipulate that wealth and all that comes with it, according to Jesus, is a major stumbling block in receiving the kingdom of God. It's going to give us fits actually. And what is the kingdom? Jesus teaches in a thousand different ways that the kingdom is later, in eternity, but the kingdom is also now, right here on earth, in the words we breathe out and the stories we live and the places God has full reign. When Jesus' ways are emulated and mercy wins, when justice rolls like a mighty river and truth is declared. Anywhere God's rule has dominion, in any moment when His way is chosen over our human instinct, His kingdom breaks through.

Jesus gave us the best glimpse into the kingdom by walking around on earth. We get to watch what this new way of living looks like, how it sounds, who it belongs to, how it is spoken, where it is willing to reach. We see that it owns very, very little but gives very, very much. We notice that it is often unsafe and wanders into dangerous territory, even if we write that off as inapplicable to us. We see the kingdom committed to unlikely folks at the bottom of the food chain; children, lepers, women, homeless people, and the way it got there was by Jesus actually going there, walking there with His feet and touching people with His hands. We watch it draw a disproportionate level of criticism from religious people; it looked very different from the hierarchy inside the temple. Its best moments were on hillsides, in rivers, around dinner tables, at funerals, on roadsides, in sick rooms, in boats—we don't actually see Jesus sequestered in the temple much.

It's this way of life, the way Jesus did it, full of courage and risk and sacrifice and back-breaking mercy that we are asked to accept.

And if He is to be believed, it is our wealth that will keep us from saying yes.

Here are the first three responses I hear when discussing these passages.

> 1. Do you mean "money" or "the love of money"?
> 2. Well, I'm not rich.
> 3. But King Solomon was rich.

I've said all three. We do not want to identify ourselves with this demographic.

Would you spend some time in humble prayer about this issue? If we have a blind spot, a very grave one according to Jesus, don't we want to know it? The first step to overcome an addiction in Alcoholics Anonymous is this: "We admit we are powerless over alcohol."[3] Admission is powerful; a necessary first step. Denial will keep us sidelined forever. Ask Jesus to speak into this. Don't be afraid. Remember: "He will not break a bruised reed, and He will not put out a smoldering wick, until He has led justice to victory" (Matt. 12:20).

What to Do at Defcon 4

Sometimes, we get to ease into things spiritually. A simple correction and everything is back on course. We need only tweak or iron out or just fine-tune a bit. The foundation is solid; only a few support beams need our attention. We see plenty of gentle correction like this in Scripture; darling passages where folks get called "my dear children" and "my dear friends" and precious things like that.

At other times biblically, the wheels come plumb off and Defcon 4 is decreed.

Certain situations simply call for urgent attention, something beyond the daily obedience of following Christ requires. The moment is too huge or the sin too great; the need is too pressing or the issue too critical. We exit "normal" and enter "crucial."

God gave us a tool for navigating these matters, something to heighten our spiritual sensitivity and perhaps expedite His intervention. We see it practiced with regularity in the Bible, but it has lost its thunder in our culture for obvious reasons. It is misunderstood and misused, neglected and forgotten.

Fasting.

According to Scripture, fasting was commanded or initiated during one of six extreme circumstances:

Mourning   Inquiry   Repentance

Preparation   Crisis   Worship

Have you ever fasted? If so, what for? What was your experience like?

Fasting is consistently practiced in Scripture, although not much is made of the mechanics, which is where we generally prefer to concentrate. Usually when discussing fasting, we major on the rules, but God didn't actually say much about those, and neither did Jesus.

It appears their primary concern was the heart of fasting, and perhaps the details were secondary. God's longest rant about fasting is in Isaiah 58 where, strangely, He condemns the outward display altogether and redirects us back to His core issues like justice and mercy and feeding the hungry.

Read Isaiah 58:1-7.

Interesting. God is definitely still calling for restraint and abstinence but not from food.

What is God begging us to refrain from here?

What does their reaction in verse 3 communicate to you?

How can you relate to this confusion?

We are not the first culture to follow God's rules but miss His heart. We've long been good on the outside. We can see in Isaiah 58 that it drives Him mad. God put the rules in place to help us find Him, help us worship, and help transform our stubborn hearts, but in a twist of irony, we perfect the mechanics and skip the pesky transformation part. It's a complicated skill set to circumvent the point altogether, but we manage to do it.

If ever you have wondered what God really cares about, let Isaiah 58 be your guidepost. If our lives are marked by gossip and slander and apathy and neglect of the poor, we can just skip all the outward disciplines and save God the energy. He is stunningly concerned with the marginalized, and He is always, always burrowing deeply into our hearts, our motives, the way we think, the reasons we move. The ax is at the root of the tree. There is a time for pruning, but sometimes a total replanting is in order.

God means business about us breaking the chains of wickedness, untying the ropes of yokes, and setting the oppressed free (see v. 6). Who and what do you think He is talking about here? Give some examples.

What would American Christians have to fast from in order to live, and I mean really live, this out?

So God endorses fasting generally but deconstructs the perfunctory practice on the basis of lingering injustice. Then we pop over to the New Testament and see Jesus address fasting with some similar contradictions, seeing how He was into it and had some ideas about doing it well. But then He totally didn't do it legalistically and people went bonkers. (It's almost like these Two care about our spiritual transformation more than obligatory obedience.)

Jesus delivers the sermon of all sermons in Matthew 5–7. He pretty much upended everything that had ever been done (oh, the dinner conversations that surely followed this subversive message).

Jesus had three sentences to say about fasting in Matthew 6:16–18. What does this passage tell you about how fasting was being observed in those days?

Jesus didn't throw the baby out with the bathwater, which I tend to do. He didn't condemn the practice of fasting altogether or tell everyone to *just forget it*, like I (allegedly) declare when my people are not performing up to my standards. He called for reform and got at the heart of the matter, not at all unlike Isaiah 58.

But there is no escaping the fact that Jesus assumes we are fasting. This isn't an "if" statement. He said: "Whenever you fast …" So there is something here worth pressing into, especially in this context of this sermon where Jesus altered a bunch of other common practices. For instance, He replaced "do not murder" with "don't even harbor anger" (see Matt. 5:21-22). "Do not commit adultery" became "don't even look at a woman lustfully" (see vv. 27-28). Jesus renovated "keep your oaths to the Lord" to "don't swear at all; just let your yes be yes and your no, no" (see vv. 33-34). He busted up "an eye for an eye" in exchange for "turn the other cheek" (see vv. 38-39). "Love your neighbor" turned into "love and pray for your enemies" (see vv. 43-44). Good gracious.

So there was precedence here for Jesus to eradicate fasting with some other superior practice. But He didn't. He kept it intact and simply addressed our intentions. There is something valuable about fasting. Jesus knew it. This is for us. This matters. This is worth keeping.

Fasting is an intentional reduction, a deliberate abstinence to summon God's movement in our lives.

A fast creates margin for God to move.

Temporarily changing our routine of comfort jars us off high-center. A fast is not necessarily something we offer God, but it assists us in offering ourselves. As Bill Bright, founder of Campus Crusade for Christ, said, "It is exchanging the needs of the physical body for those of the spiritual."[4]

By the strictest definition, fasting involves abstaining from food, but according to God in Isaiah 58, this practice can include other excesses like greed, apathy, rage, and neglect of the poor. In fact, God goes so far as to say, "Is not this the kind of fasting I have chosen?" (v. 6, NIV).

In general, how do you feel about abstaining or fasting (from food or anything else)? How do you do with restraint on the whole?

On a scale of 1-10, 1 being low and 10 being high, how would you rank yourself in terms of being disciplined?

1 2 3 4 5 6 7 8 9 10

Fasting = An Experimental Mutiny Against Excess

Let's go full circle here. God offers us fasting as a tool in extreme circumstances, which heightens our sensitivity, awareness, and His presence. It clears space for a fresh movement of the Holy Spirit. There is something mysteriously spiritual about it, and we are left trusting that God doesn't waste our time or ask for pointless compliance. The opposite is true in fact; He cannot stand empty obedience. Every word from God purposes to transform us into disciples. There is no waste, no superfluous commands. If Jesus kept fasting in the rotation, it is only because it is supremely useful. Even if we don't exactly understand what will happen in that empty space, we can trust God to meet us there. Something important awaits us.

So are we in a crisis worthy of a fast? I believe we are.

Jesus made it clear that as rich believers, even well-behaved, we have a serious blind spot. And the thing about a blind spot is, well, we're blind to it. We don't even know we can't see. This is far more insidious than our most visible sin issue. Operating with such a dangerous blind spot threatens our interpretation of Scriptures, our churches, our obedience, our role in the kingdom, our families, the suffering we're called to serve, the tasks designed for us.

If we can set our defensiveness aside and take Jesus at His word, He is pointing out our blind spot. We're a double-edged sword, privileged believers, because we are so incredibly resourced with the potential to battle disparity, but those same resources trap and tangle us, and we become unwilling to part with them. Meanwhile, the suffering happening on our watch is a tragedy while we hold all the cards. We are indulged and blind, saying *Let them eat cake* and neglecting our responsibility as privileged power-holders, redeemed gospel-bearers.

If our excess is at the root of the problem, then let's fast from it.

How do you feel about a fast from excess? Does this feel exciting? scary? Are you relieved? hopeful? cynical? What is your gut-level response?

After our Hurricane Ike guests left, I ruminated for months on this idea, letting it marinate, forcing my friends to discuss it with me. I started praying about what God wanted; what would move me closer to His agenda and further from mine? How could this fast be meaningful, not just narcissistic and futile? What areas needed the most renovation? How am I blind, and why? Where have I substituted the American Dream for God's kingdom? What in my life, in the lives of most Westerners, is just *too stinking much?*

Food   Clothes   Possessions   Media   Waste   Spending   Stress

Seven months, seven areas, reduced to seven simple choices. I embarked on a journey of less. It was time; time to purge the junk and pare down to what was necessary, what was noble. For me, 7 was an exercise in simplicity with one goal: to create space for God's kingdom to break through.

Of these seven areas, does something jump out at you? Do you relate specifically to any of these categories of excess? Why?

I approached this experiment in the spirit of a fast, which you'll remember was commanded or initiated during one of six extreme circumstances.

Mourning   Inquiry   Repentance

Preparation   Crisis   Worship

I fasted for (at least) two of these extreme reasons. First and foremost, repentance. For me, 7 was a tangible way to bow low and repent of greed, ungratefulness, ruined opportunities, and irresponsibility. It was time to admit I was trapped in the machine, held by my own selfishness. It was time to face our spending and call it what it was: a travesty. I was weary of justifying it. So many areas out of control, so much need for transformation. What were we eating? What were we doing? What had we been buying? What were we wasting? *What were we missing?* These questions grieved me, as well they should. I was ready for the deconstruction.

My second reason was for preparation. Most of my life is in front of me yet. I'm 37 years young and only a few years into my assignment as a writer and Bible teacher. The bulk of my work lies ahead. My children are young—still entirely impressionable. It is not too late to untether them from the lie of "more." Our church vision is new and our mission is really just beginning. I was hungry for the reconstruction.

Which reason(s) motivates you most to fast from your own excess? Why?

I am so glad and humbled to invite you into this story, and reader, let me tell you, it is a good story. May I drop one small spoiler alert and tell you something I learned at the close of my own experimental mutiny against excess? God did not invite me into this fast to condemn me; *it was to liberate me*. This isn't a guilt-mongering, finger-pointing, comparison game. Nor is it some angry, cynical, holier-than-thou experiment to feel superior to others.

Jesus was gentle, even in the midst of heavy deconstruction. Can I show you one more thing before we launch this little ship? In Mark's account of the rich young ruler, he includes one tiny detail the other guys left out.

Read the first sentence of Mark 10:21.

Mark isn't a mind reader. Jesus must have in some way communicated His feelings toward this rich young man, either on the spot or later.

What do you take away from this special inclusion?

Let's close with this grand finale. This is how the story wraps up.

"[The disciples] were even more astonished, saying to one another, 'Then who can be saved?' Looking at them, Jesus said, 'With men it is impossible, but not with God, because all things are possible with God.'" Mark 10:26–27

Oh, blessed relief! Folks, we can use all our engineering smarts and genetic modifications and sleight of hands and brute strength, and we will still be unable to shove that camel through the eye of the needle. It is, as Jesus said, impossible. The camel is too big and clunky and no human effort can force him through.

But with exactitude and grace and power untold, God can do this. Somehow, He is able to thread that needle with precision, using the most unwieldy material. God can give us eyes to see and ears to hear; He can gift us with perspective and wisdom, discernment and mercy. These are His to disperse, and they change everything. In His care, luxuries can become disposable and resources dispensable. Hearts of stone become flesh; it is a miracle every time. No one is beyond His reach.

Not even me.

Not even you.

There is hope for us camels on this side of the needle; Jesus looks at us and loves us.

It is supremely important to get your head right before a fast. Take as long as you need to work this out with Jesus. Fasting for the wrong reasons is just narcissistic. This doesn't mean you need to have all your junk together ... hardly! You can come a hot mess like we all are, but come for Jesus. Come for transformation. Come for worship. Come humble and honest, open and listening.

Don't feel this way yet? Pray for it. Ask God to prepare you and render your heart willing. Ask about those blind spots. Put it all out there. Jesus can handle every bit of your honesty.

Week 2

FOOD

Video Notes

Group Guide

Does your lifestyle influence your food choices or do your food choices influence your lifestyle? Why?

How could food become an idol in our lives that distracts us from God's kingdom?

What are some practical ways you can live out Jesus' words in Matthew 25:35-40?

Video session downloads available at www.lifeway.com/jenhatmaker

Getting Ready for Food

We'll get into it at length, but first things first: It's time to pick your poison for this first week of *The 7 Experiment*. I'm super anxious about not turning this into a burden. Any time we attempt abstinence or restraint, it's a slippery slope straight into legalism. It's just our nature.

As we are operating in the spirit of a fast rather than the letter of the law, let me throw out some options for you this week. There are plenty of means to the same end; this isn't a competition or comparison game. Nor is there a formula or template. There is a reason God only spoke of our motives in fasting rather than the mechanics, and He can render our hearts in all sorts of ways.

In my own 7 experiment, I chose seven foods I would eat for the month (and you only have to figure this out for one week, lucky ducks). I consulted experts and Web sites and less-skilled advisors like my girlfriends. I studied some trustworthy nutrition Web sites to determine healthy ratios of vitamins and minerals.[1] I researched super foods and organic produce. I prayed over my choices and these were the finalists.

Chicken   Eggs

Whole wheat bread   Sweet potatoes

Spinach   Avocados   Apples

I only drank water (noooooooo coffeeeeeeee, boooooooo), and I used olive oil, salt, and pepper in modest increments. The end.

If you'd like to take the route of seven foods for a week, make sure your choices are healthy and balanced. Whole foods are best (don't get me started on the bread I chose; it had 28 ingredients … fail). You *gotta* have some fruits and veggies in there. Just eat like a smart person. This is a good time to leave off chocolate ice cream, potato chips, and candy bars.

Here are some alternative options for this week:

- Cut out seven ingredients. For instance, no foods with high fructose corn syrup, caffeine, sugar, white flour, alcohol, food dye, and/or partially hydrogenated oil.
- No fast food or processed food; only whole foods (this is harder than you think).
- Feel burdened for a specific country? Eat their simple diet for seven days.
- Eat the same simple breakfast, lunch, and dinner every day.
- Eliminate seven favorite go-to foods.
- Eat what you already have; no grocery shopping. Figure out how to use freezer, pantry, and fridge ingredients you've already bought.
- Cut your weekly grocery budget in half (or in third!). Experience more deliberate, simple eating and give the savings away.
- Fast entirely from one meal a day, creating seven opportunities to pray and diligently seek Jesus.

In my family, we exempted the kids from this section, although their menu for the month was greatly simplified. Our food limitations were just harder to transfer to them for an entire month. Figure out what works for you and your family; no hard rules here. Some versions lend themselves to kid inclusion, and some are trickier.

After discussing with your spouse, family, roommates, or partners in crime, how have you decided to fast from food this week?

What are your concerns?

More is More and Other Nonsense

When my book 7 was first released, I engaged a whirlwind of radio and media interviews. Nothing like calling in for a live broadcast in your cut-off sweat shorts, messy bun, and bare feet, pretending to be a professional. (I've called in while pulled over on the side of the road with my hazards on, squatting under a tree during a motorcycle ride, locked in a hotel vending room blocking the door with my foot in case someone needed ice, and from a Barnes and Noble bathroom. Classy.)

Most of these interviews were lovely. *Most.*

During one live interview with two older gentlemen who, let's just say didn't exactly fit my target demographic, I basically endured their nonstop criticism for a book they'd never even cracked open. They probably glanced at the press release three minutes before our interview, and—as one of them told me *on air*—"figured it was one of those self-published books on account o' that cover."

Awesome.

As I was digging deep for graciousness and poise (while my Facebook friends were listening in, lighting up my page with outrage and hilarity), one of the hosts let out a big sigh and said:

"What is this even all about? *More is more.* Am I right? You can't tell me I'm not right. You'd rather us starve?"

And this was a national Christian program … sigh.

As we enter this first week of fasting together, dear reader, may I gently suggest that when it comes to food, more is not always more? That position netted us an unprecedented national health epidemic. No country has ever been this sick, this fat, and this diseased based on a toxic food supply and bad choices. But I'm getting ahead of myself.

Preparing for this month of 7, I counted how many food items I had in my pantry, refrigerator, and freezer: 240. Would you kindly go count how many food items you have?

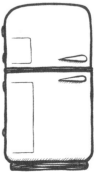

Have you or your family members ever stood in your kitchen and declared there was nothing to eat? I cannot tell you how often I've said and heard that. Worse yet is the amount of food we threw away that we never got around to eating, because we simply had too many choices. Of course, we pitched tons of perfectly good leftovers, because why eat yesterday's food when we could have new food, am I right? You can't tell me I'm not right. More is more. (Pardon me. I frequently lapse into sarcasm.)

When it comes to fasting, food is the common focus. The noun translated "fast" or "a fasting" is *tsom* in Hebrew and *nesteia* in Greek. It means the voluntary abstinence from food. The literal Hebrew translation is "not to eat." The literal Greek means "no food." Though the spirit of fasting is much broader, as God clearly pointed out in Isaiah 58 and as we will employ elsewhere, food is the letter of the law here.

And let me tell you: There is a bunch of gobbledygook out there on fasting from food, which is interesting, because the Bible is actually very sparse on the mechanics. A quick Google search reveals our obsession with the details rather than the heart of abstinence leading to communion. *How many days? What can I have? Are there loopholes? What is the perfect number? What if this? What if that?*

Originally, only one day of fasting was required in the law, on the Day of Atonement. By the end of the Old Testament period, three other days had been added throughout the course of a year. Each fast was just one day long.

Outside those required fasts, others were initiated on a need basis. They were recorded as 1 day, 3 days, 7 days, several days, 21 days, and the longest at 40 days, which Jesus went through. When done in obedience, God responded to them all, so His history declares that He does not have a magic number.

In addition to these, Scripture describes a couple of partial fasts (like we are engaging this week in one form or another). Technically, humanity started with a partial fast: You two can eat any plants, any at all … except this one. Oops. Our best example is probably Daniel and his three Jewish friends who ate only fruits, vegetables, and water for 10 days (then later for 3 weeks). They had the choicest food at their disposal, so we have much in common with this particular account. Worth noting, the Bible records the specific health benefits.

 *"At the end of 10 days they looked better and healthier than all the young men who were eating the king's food. So the guard continued to remove their food and the wine they were to drink and gave them vegetables." Daniel 1:15-16*

Has fasting ever been a part of your spiritual story? If so, how has God moved in you through this obedience?

If not, what kept you from fasting? Confusion? Misunderstanding? Fear? Explain your hesitancy.

It's interesting to watch God's movement after the famous fasts in Scripture; they positioned His people for a breakthrough so often. What wasn't possible, suddenly was. What wouldn't move, came unstuck. What hadn't worked, finally did. What was totally blurry, became crystal clear.

Esther and her attendants fasted for three days before she approached the king without being summoned, a death sentence; yet he welcomed her and Israel was saved from extinction (see Esth. 4:16). When Ezra was carrying a large consignment of gold and silver to the temple along a route infested with pillagers, he fasted for protection; they arrived safely in Jerusalem (see Ezra 8:21-23). Daniel fasted for revelation from God on restoring Jerusalem after almost 70 years in exile, and God sent the angel Gabriel to describe His wonderful plan of redemption (see Dan. 9:3,20-21). The Antioch church was fasting in worship, and God told them to anoint Paul and Barnabas "for the work I have called them to" (Acts 13:2). Let's just stipulate *that* worked out.

When three nations waged war against Judah, King Jehoshaphat called for a nationwide fast for spiritual direction. I particularly love this story.

Read 2 Chronicles 20:1-30. What beautiful elements of fasting do you pick up on here? List everything you notice.

Specifically in the area of excess and indulgence, are you in need of a breakthrough? What difficult or seemingly impossible circumstances face you?

Let it be said, we cannot use fasting to manipulate God to give us what we want. David fasted for the life of his baby, but the consequences of his sin against Bathsheba and Uriah ran its course (see 2 Sam. 12:16-23). A group of Jews in Acts tried to get God on their side to kill Paul after his Jesus yammering. "The Jews formed a conspiracy and bound themselves under a curse: neither to eat nor to drink until they had killed Paul" (Acts 23:12), yet Paul was spared. And God told His people all throughout the Old Testament that their fasting moved Him not one iota because their hearts were far from Him.

This is a good time to check motives here. Write a brief prayer telling God what you're hoping for during this fast. (This was my summary: God, may there be less of me and my junk, and more of You and Your kingdom.)

If you are struggling with your intentions, that's OK. Just be honest. Ask God to move you toward His heart, maybe something as simple as "Help me care."

What is a Gogurt?

Occasionally I come across a book that is so insightful, it is a real struggle not to plagiarize the entire thing. If I could insert the entire content of *In Defense of Food* right here, I would do it. It has revolutionized my ideas about food and nutrition. This is the main premise: Eat food. Not too much. Mostly plants.

What author Michael Pollan means by "food" is "real food" that came from the ground, a tree, a plant, or an animal without messing with it; food that hasn't been loaded with corn syrup or injected with hormones. He writes not as a nutritionist overcomplicating something simple but writes on the authority of tradition and common sense.

> By the 1960s or so it had become all but impossible to sustain tradi-tional ways of eating in the face of the industrialization of our food. If you wanted to eat produce grown without synthetic chemicals or meat raised on pasture without pharmaceuticals, you were out of luck. The supermarket had become the only place to buy food, and real food was rapidly disappearing from its shelves, to be replaced by the modern cornucopia of highly processed foodlike products.[2]

Our grandmas ate local meat and vegetables from their gardens; we eat boxed pastries we bulk-ordered online. Today in America, the culture of food is changing more than once a generation, which is historically unprecedented. This machine is driven by a 32 billion-dollar food-marketing engine that thrives on change for its own sake, not to mention constantly shifting nutri-tional science that keeps folding in on itself every few years.

> Like a large gray cloud, a great Conspiracy of Scientific Complexity has gathered around the simplest questions of nutrition—much to the advantage of everyone involved. Expect perhaps the supposed beneficiary of all this nutritional advice: us, and our health and happiness as eaters. For the most important thing to know about the campaign to profes-sionalize dietary advice is that it has not made us any healthier. To the contrary: it has actually made us less healthy and considerably fatter.[3]

Clearly. Four of the top 10 causes of death today are chronic diseases with well-established links to our industrialized diet: coronary heart disease, stroke, diabetes, and cancer.[4] These health plagues remain rare in countries where people don't eat like us, even if its local diet is high in fat or carbs—the two straw men America decided to fight.

The basics of the Western diet include:
- Rise of highly processed foods and refined grains
- Use of chemicals to raise plants and animals in huge monocultures
- Abundance of cheap calories of sugar and fat
- Massive consumption of fast food
- Shrinking diversity of the human diet to a tiny handful of subsidized staple crops, notably wheat, corn, and soy
- Conspicuous absence of fruit, vegetables, and whole grains.[5]

This bodes terribly for us, and it is downright disastrous for our children. In fact, U.S. life expectancy was projected to rise indefinitely, but new data from the New England Journal of Medicine suggests this trend is about to reverse itself due to the rapid rise in obesity, especially among children. Our kids are the first generation in the history of America that has a shorter life span than their parents.[6]

Do you struggle with any elements of the Western diet listed in this discussion? If so, which ones and why?

How have we come to this point in food history? A recent documentary on the industrialization of food production reveals some staggering facts. Processed foods, including meats and produce, deliver profoundly less nutrition to us but more profits to the companies producing them. Though these corporations boast of efficiency, they also depart from original farming techniques that proved successful in keeping our ancestors alive and well for generations.[7]

Some Light Reading from Leviticus (sarcasm)

The way we eat has changed in the last 50 years. Which brings me back to God (see what I did there?). He actually thought about food and how to feed us well. We're not going to find a cautionary tale against Spam in Scripture, because only Westerners could come up with something so unnatural, but we do find some very interesting and helpful food guidelines in God's Word.

First of all, at the very beginning, God told Adam and Eve this: "I have given you every seed-bearing plant on the surface of the entire earth and every tree whose fruit contains seed. This food will be for you" (Gen. 1:29). Thank You, Lord, for making wheat a seed-bearing plant. Bread = good. So He launched humanity as vegans, and they stayed this way for some time.

After the flood, God told Noah: "The fear and terror of you will be in every living creature on the earth, every bird of the sky, every creature that crawls on the ground, and all the fish of the sea. They are placed under your authority. Every living creature will be food for you; as I gave the green plants, I have given you everything" (Gen. 9:2-3). This was a good inclusion at this point, since all the vegetation was, well, drowned.

OK, so now meat is fine. Well, not all meat.

God delineated between clean and unclean meat early on, because He told Noah to bring seven pairs of every type of clean animal (for mating, eating, and sacrificing, as only "clean animals" have ever been acceptable as a spiritual offering) but just one pair of unclean animals for the procreation of their species (see Gen. 7:2). Noah seemed to understand this distinction perfectly.

God got serious about recording specifics in the Law, both in Leviticus 11 and Deuteronomy 14. Take a deep breath and read Leviticus 11. As you read, note the basic rule of thumb God established for each of the following animal groups.

Animals that live on land (vv. 2-8) _____

Animals that live in water (vv. 9-12) _____

Birds (vv. 13-19) _____

Flying insects (vs. 20-23) _____

Animals that move along the ground (vv. 29-31,41-44) _____

It's interesting to assess the Law, outlined in the first five books of the Bible, through the layers of history upon it and realize what foresight God displayed. *Halley's Bible Handbook* states: "Moses' Law [including] its health and food regulations, was far purer, more rational, humane … and showed a wisdom far in advance of, anything in ancient legislation, Babylonian, Egyptian or any other."[8] So many regulations protected the Hebrews from disease, contamination, infection, illness, sexual defilement, family ruin, estate loss, injustice, civil unrest, and anarchy. (Still today, we see millions of people dying from contaminated water, diseased food, and unsanitary practices forbidden in Scripture.)

In many ways, the Law established harmonious society and general goodwill, calling for the canceling of debts, care of the widow and alien, love for your brother, civil justice, and equity toward servants. God explained how to treat the earth so it would continue to yield its bounty, giving it a year of respite every seven years; basic agricultural science. He provided for food storage and communal redistribution, cities of refuge and cycles of rest, military infrastructure and dispute resolutions. He considered everything people needed for well-being, life, community, and worship and laid it out with precision.

From this health, civility, and best practices standpoint, God's food rules make all kinds of sense and are supported by every common sense nutritional advocate today. I don't see many dieticians saying, "You know what we need in America? Less green leafy vegetables and way more processed bacon."

What standard healthy principles do you notice in the clean foods God approved for consumption?

Hilarious that "grass-fed beef" is all the rage today; this is, um, the way it was always supposed to be. An animal that "chews the cud" simply re-chews plant foods that it has already partially digested in some way. This method of nutrient absorption extracts the ultimate benefit from nutrient-poor vegetation like grass and leaves. Most clean animals are herbivores, whereas most unclean animals are carnivores. The two-part prescription included hooved feet, which disqualified certain animals. These two texts specifically condemned pigs, camels, the coney (rock badger), and rabbits.

Generally, God forbid the consumption of scavengers, predators, and bottom-dwellers. To be sure, these animals serve important roles in ecological cycles as the Environmental Clean-Up Crew of sorts, capable of ingesting and processing tremendous amounts of poison and waste in short periods of time.

Some scavengers, like catfish, crabs, and lobsters, are bottom-feeders. Clams and oysters are filter feeders that purify water by concentrating chemicals and bacteria in their tissues. Others, like vultures and crows, eat dead, rotting flesh. This assists in the breakdown of organic matter and bacteria, so they do not remain toxic to the environment. Hogs actually have specially designed pus ducts located above their hooves to regularly drain poisons from their bodies. Obviously, these animals are ridden with toxins, parasites, and pathogens; great for the earth, terrible for our bodies. By abstaining from these unclean animals, we do not rid the planet of its necessary clean-up crew, nor do we ingest the toxins they were created to filter.

God is protecting His entire creation.

Based on these basic principles, in summary, what sort of diet did God design for His people?

It goes without saying these plants and animals were seasonal, local, and organic. (What else was there?) We are what we eat, and we are what they eat. I believe if God considered an animal unclean simply for eating other animals in the wild, He probably frowns upon fattening cattle for slaughter with corn, synthetic growth hormones, and antibiotics. I'm guessing He isn't down with a poultry industry that feeds chickens rendered animal parts banned from bovine and human consumption, living and breathing in their own excrement with less than half a square foot to move within cages in factory farms. It may not be in our best interests to ingest processed "chicken" nuggets.

Nor can I imagine a divine endorsement of the chemicals, preservatives, synthetic fillers, sweeteners, artificial flavors, factory-created fats, and colorings added to processed food while stripping it of its natural nutrients, rendering it just *a hot mess*. Most of what we find in the grocery store isn't even food, y'all. It's fake food, held together by scandalous standards ("Sugar-Laden Cereal! Heart Healthy!"), and a suspension of good, old-fashioned common sense by busy consumers seduced into convenience shopping. When we have "guacamole dip" with the teeny tiny disclaimer—*does not contain actual avocados*—we have a problem, folks.

This might defy the whole food, farm-to-table system God designed for us.

What drives your food choices most?

What connection do you recognize between what you eat and feed your family and how God created a healthy food supply? Or do you keep "God's best practices" and "what we eat" in two separate containers? Explain.

Bulls, Bells, and Bodies

Scripture is full of the symbolism between the original temple in the old covenant and the new temple—our bodies—under the new covenant. It's a stunning word picture: the holy of holies where the presence of God dwelt, housed in the ark of the covenant behind a large curtain, the innermost sanctuary of the temple. Only the high priest—and only once a year (the required day of fasting)—could enter to offer a sacrifice of atonement for the nation's sins. And this was no simple matter of shoving the curtain aside and sprinkling a little blood around. This sacrifice was so sacred, God gave over 100 directives on how it had to be done.

Including the sacrifice of *clean animals*: "Present a burnt offering to the LORD, a pleasing aroma: one young bull, one ram, and seven male lambs a year old. All your animals are to be unblemished" (Num. 29:8).

In fact, in case one element was offensive, God commanded of the hem of the high priest's robe: "Make pomegranates of blue, purple, and scarlet yarn on its lower hem and all around it. Put gold bells between them all the way around. The robe must be worn by Aaron whenever he ministers, and its sound will be heard when he enters the sanctuary before the LORD and when he exits, so that he does not die" (Ex. 28:33,35). In other words, if the worship was tainted, the high priest would be struck instantly dead, and the other priests would know by the silence of the bells.

God is holy. So very holy. We have no concept how holy and perfect He is. That God could even be close to sinful mankind is astonishing, which is why it was so complicated to bring worship that wouldn't offend His perfection.

He is still that holy. Which brings us to Jesus.

Read of the moment Jesus died on the cross in Mark 15:37–38. How did Jesus' sacrifice forever change worship from how it had been since its inception?

Read 1 Corinthians 3:16–17. Jesus changed the parameters of the temple, but do you think He changed its sanctity? Are our bodies more or less sacred? Explain.

How do you think God's immense concern over every detail of the original temple translates to how He wants us to manage our bodies, the new temple?

Rather than the blood of lambs, goats, rams, and bulls, we are now cleansed through the blood of Jesus; the Spirit indwells. We are the royal priesthood, bearers of the holy place within. The veil is torn. We are sacred, hallowed through Jesus.

It's almost too beautiful to handle.

True Christianity is certainly more than eating and drinking, but it may be wise to consider that God desires for us to exercise stewardship over our bodies just as He expects stewardship of our resources. Maybe housing the Spirit of God is still holy territory. Do our bodies boast of sacred content? Do we treat our bodies like vessels of the very presence of the great I AM? Is there a remnant of respect and reverence for these bodies, and these plants and animals consecrated for our sustenance?

Or do we casually fuel our earthly temples with chemicals, synthetic hormones, poisons, and pathogens, ignoring every alarm screaming how sick, obese, unwell, and diseased we are? I know I have suspended the connection between my body and the Spirit who lives in it. I've asked Jesus, "Present my body a living sacrifice to You, holy and pleasing? Well, You can have my mind, my heart, and even my hands, but I'd like to keep the actual body to myself, thank You. I'm sure You won't mind. I'm sure You didn't even mean that."

How would God find you treating your body and your family's bodies today? In what ways would He commend your choices? What concerns might He have?

Listen, this is not about being skinny or sculpting some perfect body. Because we are so fat and unhealthy here in the Land of Meat Containing Meatlike Products, it's hard to consider this discussion properly, which should elevate *health* over *weight*. I mean, we are the same people who consume fatty foods made with a cooking oil which prevents absorption, so we can have our chips and eat them too, because rather than pesky weight gain, we'll just have spontaneous diarrhea.

Our thinking on nutrition is so crazy and faulty and foolish and lazy (why eat healthy, clean, whole foods when we could just sprinkle "magic drops" on our potato skins and lose weight while we sleep?), we've disconnected entirely from the correct objective: health.

This is my one life. God chose these few years for my turn on earth. This is it. This is the heart He gave me, created to carry me through my tasks. I'm counting on these lungs to tell of His goodness, to sing my worship, to mother my children, to speak good news. These hands have much work to do. This is the vessel God gave me to tell His story, to love His people, to champion the kingdom. He gave us best practices in Scripture and said, "put these things in your heart, put these things in your mind, put these things in your mouth … trust Me." These truths, these visions, this nourishment; they cohabitate with the Spirit inside us.

These temples house so much of value.

How does your life reveal the value you place on the body God has given you with which you're called to serve Him?

In what areas, along with food, can we honor God with our bodies?

Is it possible God's ideas on food are not there to weigh us down but increase our quality of life? Could He simply be protecting our health, a God ever *for us*? Is He pleased when we treat our bodies like the temples Jesus transformed them into? Are these clean sacrifices still a pleasing aroma unto Him?

God used the physical body of Jesus to save the world; "This is My body, which is given for you. Do this in remembrance of Me" (Luke 22:19). If Jesus yielded His body for the salvation of mankind, good readers, maybe we should offer ours too, a sacrifice of thanksgiving; strong, nourished, well-tended, ready, capable of living and working and moving and executing the heavy lifting of the gospel, prepared to extend our last living breath for the glory of Jesus and the beauty of His kingdom.

Your kingdom come, Your will be done on earth as it is in heaven. Here are our hands, our hearts, our bodies, our lives. Use us, expend us till the end of our days, for we are Yours.

Need to do business with God in this area? Say what you need to say. We are dangerously misguided in this department, I fear. Wrestle, ask questions, grieve, be still. God cares about this immensely. He cares for you.

Want more? Here are some potential action steps:

- Find your community's farmer's market and hit it up. Meet some of your local farmers. Spend your chow budget on local, organic, fresh food.
- Resolve to cook. Processed convenience food is, well, convenient. Real food requires chopping, sautéing, grilling, cooking. This takes planning, diligence, and often working ahead of time. We can do this. People lived like this for thousands of years.
- Find out if your area has a CSA to join (Community Supported Agriculture). You get a share of their produce weekly or bimonthly for a set fee. If you're lucky like me, you can also buy fresh eggs and fair-trade coffee from them.

- Need help getting over yourself in this department? Spend some time with the truly hungry. Volunteer at your local food bank, a local homeless shelter/kitchen at mealtime, pack a bunch of sandwiches and take them to folks on street corners.
- Go through your fridge and pantry, and get rid of all the toxic junk. Or if that feels too radical, just finish eating it and make up your mind to not replace it. Think of this as worship, because it is. You are respecting God, His creation, and the food system He kindly put in place to nourish us.

Wrap Up

May I share with you my personal response at the close of my 7 food fast?

It's the last day of Month One, and I have some conclusions. I'm grateful food launched me out of the starting blocks. There was no shirking possible, no viable semi-attention. Seven foods required my concentration from morning until night, every day. Each meal was intentional, each bite calculated. There was no escape from 7; I never had longer than five hours between meals to mentally slip away. The concept of reduction was never further than my next meal.

This held me fast to the heart of Jesus.

Just as a forty-day fast inaugurated His public ministry, this month has paved the way. It's gently erased parts of the palette. I don't know nearly as much as I think I do. My riches aren't genuine. My story includes some fraud. Certain elements don't belong on the canvas. I don't know what this means yet, but the counterfeit parts must be whitewashed before they can be redrawn. ...

My mission is clouded by a thousand elements with no eternal value. The canvas is muddy. I know the correct Christian rhetoric—emptiness, surrender, humility—but those words are meaningless until they are more than words. While my life is marked by ambition, accumulation, and perceived success, then no matter how much I squawk about Jesus, I'm a resounding gong, a clanging symbol; I am nothing.

After Jesus' fast, He began healing, rescuing, redeeming. The Spirit filled up the emptiness Jesus created, launching Him into ministry. In some supernatural way, the abstinence from food was the catalyst for Jesus' unveiling; the real fireworks were next. Never again would Jesus fly under the radar. His powerful ministry was activated, inviting worship and opposition, salvation and death. After thirty years on earth, His story truly began.

"He ate nothing during those days, and at the end of them he was hungry" (Luke 4:2, NIV).

I am hungry.[9]

How did your fast from food go this week? What did you learn about yourself? What did you notice about your habits? What was difficult? What was surprising? How did God speak in the empty space? Any breakthroughs? Any disappointments? What will you take away?

Week 3

CLOTHING

Video Notes

Group Guide

Why do you think we spend so much time consumed with our clothes?

How might your closet reflect your heart?

Read Matthew 6:21. How have you found Jesus' words true in your life?

Read Matthew 6:28-30. How can Jesus' words encourage you when it comes to your closet?

Video session downloads available at www.lifeway.com/jenhatmaker

Getting Ready for Clothes

We'll get down to the nitty-gritty in Scripture this week, because there is plenty in there about clothes and adornment and nakedness and stuff, but before we start, it's time to decide what your clothes fast will look like.

Again, we are hedging with the spirit of the law rather than the letter, so there is plenty of wiggle room here. Because we value our wardrobes differently, one person's fast is another's average Tuesday. Some of us need a work ensemble and others don't. Some need to include exercise clothes, and others prefer to watch television on our couch with chips and salsa (I've heard). I encourage you to choose a path that will pinch—a fast is supposed to be uncomfortable; that is where the magic happens.

In my own 7 experiment, I chose seven clothes for one month.

One pair of jeans, dark wash, kind of plain

One long-sleeved solid black T-shirt, fitted

One short-sleeved black "Haiti relief" T-shirt with white print

One short-sleeved gray "Mellow Johnny's Bike Shop" T-shirt with yellow print

One pair of gray drawstring knit Capri pants

One long silk dark brown dress shirt (my "speaker shirt")

Shoes: cowboy boots and tennis shoes*

* Shoes counted as one item. However, I only rotated through two pairs of shoes: my cowboy boots and my tennis shoes. I had to reconcile my stay home life with my Conference Speaker life, and I'm sorry, but I wasn't wearing nice cowboy boots with my yoga pants to the park.

** Underwear didn't count. It just didn't, OK?

*** I also omitted all jewelry (except my wedding ring) and accessories. TEAR.

**** Our kids got a free pass on this one, because I didn't want to answer to their therapists on why I made them wear the same seven clothes for a month of fourth grade. *Thank you for understanding.* However, in hindsight, I should've given them a version of the project for the month. (I didn't know what I was doing, OK? I was so happy to have coffee back that I couldn't think straight.)

If you'd like to take the seven clothes route, which I assure you is doable for seven days, check your calendar and include necessary items for your schedule this week. If you have to wear it, you have to count it. Wait, that sounded bossy. How about: If you have to wear something specific this week, you should count it as one of your choices. (Better?)

Here are some alternatives for this week, or feel free to invent your own:

- Grab a small bag (like a reusable grocery store bag). Whatever fits in there, including shoes, is what you have for the week. Shut your closet door and live out of the bag.
- Seven clothes too easy? Make undergarments and shoes count as individual items.
- Wear the same shirt all week but rotate pants (or vice versa).
- Wear the same outfit all week, but change your accessories each day.
- Choose seven items to wear every day, but find a way to wear them differently; one outfit, seven ways.

- Ladies, in a similar "outward appearance" thread, reduce your toiletries to only seven items, including makeup. For instance: shampoo, conditioner, one hair product, moisturizer, foundation, mascara, and lip gloss.
- You could give yourself a seven-minute time limit on getting ready each morning after your shower. (Easy for some, impossible for others.)
- Wear only clothes you haven't worn in over a year, even shoes.

Again, if you're a parent, it's totally up to you on including your kids. If they are up for the adventure, go for it. If they are too little or too self-conscious or too whiny (is that just mine?), feel free to exempt them. I've been pleasantly surprised at feedback from parents whose kiddos jumped into the deep end with them. You might be amazed what your young ones are up for.

After discussing with your spouse, family, roommates, or partners in crime, how have you decided to fast from clothes this week?

What are your concerns?

Fake Correspondence from Humble Island

The first time I became aware of clothes was middle school. Up until then, I was a fashion tragedy with no concept of style. But in sixth grade, words like Forenza and Outback Red and Esprit and Guess made their way into my vernacular, if not my closet.

Please try to remember sixth grade, especially if you are a girl. Recall the cruel awkwardness, the certainty you were tipping the scales at 95 pounds, and the fear no boy would ever get past your home perm. Remember how all your friends wore Guess jeans, and your mom said she'd rather book a one-way ticket to commie Russia before shelling out $50 for jeans? (I was a tragic 12-year-old stuck in lower middle class during the Cold War.)

Incidentally, I recently chaperoned a middle school dance where my oldest two attend. It is both horrifying and refreshing that *nothing* has changed. Because I care about edifying the world, I composed a series of live-tweets from the #MSdance.

> The cool kid is rallying everyone (the girls) to the dance floor. He is adorbs. He should have his own show on the Disney Channel. #MSdance

> These awkward boys … bless it. I'm going to ask them to dance. Wait, never mind. I'm 25 years too old for that to be helpful. #MSdance

> Fighting the urge to pull a few of these tragic girls aside & assure them IT GETS BETTER. These are not your best years, punkins. #MSdance

> Ladies and gentlemen, we have a Dance Circle. It's like a scene from *Step Up 2*, but with way less talent. #MSdance

> True story: DJ is busting out a Michael Jackson montage. It's like he is daring me to join the Dance Circle. #MSdance

> Pull your pants up. Your pants are too small. Pull your shirt down. Get your hair out of your eyes. #somethingsiwanttosay #MSdance

I just told an awkward boy who has been sitting near me the whole time: "Don't worry. You're going to be rich & successful." #MSdance

I am so sorry to tell you we are in the final 10 minutes of our #MSdance. These kids can save their sob stories. I had a home perm.

In so many ways, the horrible compulsion to fit in, to be noticed, to fancy up the outside remains, doesn't it? You think middle school was tough? Try Mommy Wars. You'll pull back a nub.

I used to claim outsider's status on these competitive circles: Oh, I don't care about that stuff, I said. I'm comfortable in my own skin. Those things don't hold value for me. I don't care about clothes and fancy shoes and looking awesome and impressing people. I just love Jesus and kittens and live over here on Humble Island.

Then I started my clothes fast for 7 and accidentally totaled how many items of clothes I had in my closet including shoes, scarves, and belts: 327. This affirmed my eviction from Humble Island—extinguish your torch, the tribe has spoken, and it says you're a hypocritical liar. Good-bye now.

It's good to know real numbers. Our perceptions prop things up and trick us. How many items of clothes would you guess you have?

Would you go count? How many clothes do you actually have?

Let's resist the urge to compare here. I have three times as many clothes as some of you, and others have three times as many as me. We will derail this discussion with comparison, either commending ourselves for being more frugal or languishing in guilt for being less. Either way, we will miss the point. We have different stories and different backgrounds and different contexts, so let's just make this about ourselves and not anyone else. As MJ told us, of #MSdance montage fame: "I'm starting with the man in the mirror ..."

I find the discussion on clothes in most Christian circles to be contextually irrelevant, isolating, and superficial. Most spiritual leaders on this topic major on modesty. Or dressing up for church versus not dressing up for church. Or low-cut shirts. Or miniskirts. (Precious little is directed at men, mind you.) This concept is often reduced to a shame-based lecture against women while entirely ignoring the more glaring issues. Like Jesus said so eloquently when addressing this concern and more to the Pharisees:

"Blind guides! You strain out a gnat, yet gulp down a camel!" Matthew 23:24

Very few spiritual leaders seem concerned over how much we spend on fashion, or the bondage we are in to public opinion, or how many of our clothes are made by the hands of children and slaves, or how fashion is a trite, insulting topic globally, or how Jesus told us to clothe the naked and quit showing favoritism to the well-heeled and clean the inside rather than spit-polish the outside. It is reduced to a moral issue, excused from being an injustice issue.

So if you don't mind me skipping the parts where I tell you to stop wearing sequined tube tops and walking around and causing men to stumble (women) or falling helplessly prey to these loose women (men), may we dive into a deeper discussion together, confronting the elephants in the dressing room?

Popular

Let's start with economic disparity. Sound fun? (Wouldn't this be easier if I just told you not to wear short shorts? Seriously, men. Stop doing that.) Clothes have always been an outward indicator of social inequity. *How much is too much?* is only a "problem" rich people wrestle with. If you've ever watched children in a developing country run around in tattered rags, the only set of clothes they own, you realize that in the big picture, this is a very banal discussion.

James did a great job laying it bare.

Read James 2:1-6.

What does James suggest a super well-dressed person triggers in other people, even believers? How about a poorly dressed person? Explain your thoughts on these two reactions.

This is a secular response that long ago bled over to the saints. We see inherent value in the well-heeled, implied disgrace in the poorly outfitted. Our default reaction favors the smart dresser, assigning him or her a whole set of positive attributes that may or may not be purely imaginary. We make an enormous leap in half a second, developing an entire character sketch on appearance. And with a bias toward the top of the food chain, let's be honest: it behooves us to hobnob with those above our rung. Our chances for upward mobility increase dramatically.

James highlights this reaction by not commenting on this rich man's character at all but simply addressing the believers' response to him. The early church was predominantly poor, so if a rich man graced their presence, it must have been a real temptation to make a fuss over him. (Totally still happens. Is it any wonder that church boards are filled with the wealthiest, most successful businessmen?)

Continue reading verses 7-13. James cautions us against judgment without mercy, particularly in the context of perceived social distinctions. How do you assess other people based on what they are wearing? It's OK to be honest.

Have you ever showed favoritism based on someone's appearance? What were the circumstances? Or maybe the flip side: have you discredited or ignored someone because of his or her poor appearance? Talk about this.

Not only do we apply this worth assessment to others based on what they are wearing, we direct it toward ourselves. As modern American believers, we find ourselves in the interesting position of being both the rich man and the believer in this story. Though James warned us off such a conclusion, we've bought into it: *My clothes say something important about me.* I can draw the eye. I could be shown the special attention. I could get the good seat.

To be clear: There is nothing wrong with beauty, so let's not fuel that drama. We have Rachel and Esther and David and Solomon, all noted for their beauty and style. Plus, God seeded so many of us with flair and creativity, and clothes are often an outward expression of our personalities, an extension of our gifts. And we have to get dressed, so ...

But like any necessary thing, the tail can so easily wag the dog here. We have to eat, but food is so readily abused, we find ourselves sick, overweight, obsessed, and unhealthy. God created sex as a beautiful expression, but need we discuss how we've exploited this gift? Influence, authority, wealth, position, ecological resources, power, biblical knowledge ... all gifts, all capable of heinous misuse.

Complete this sentence: What my clothes communicate (or what I want them to communicate) about me is ...

God makes it clear that outward appearance and inward truth are sometimes two totally different things. Is there a discrepancy between the message you want to send about yourself and your true motives? Explain.

My "Need" for Bleach Pens

Back to economics. Let's get serious here. I walked through all our closets and realized we spent real cash on every single item. I did some fuzzy averaging, and if we spent around $10 on each item, our closets represent an expenditure of, well, a lot of money (I'm a writer not an accountant). It is such a high total I had to sit down. Especially considering we don't wear half of the items.

And let's be honest, for my 327 items, most didn't average $10. If I spent $20 on each item, that was $6,540 spent on just my clothes in about the last five years. If the average is closer to $30, that means I spent $9,810. This didn't include anyone else in the family.

Sadly, I only wore a tiny percentage of these clothes. So while my mouth was proclaiming my laissez-faire attitude toward my wardrobe, my hand kept reaching into my wallet to buy more. If I was serious about addressing over-indulgence and irresponsible spending, I need not look any further than our closets. I spent more just on clothes in one year than the average Ethiopian family earns in almost five.

Read Matthew 6:28-30. Why do you think our culture spends so much time, energy, and money on clothing? What could this indicate about our faith (as Jesus makes a clear link between the two)?

It is shockingly easy to disconnect the way we spend with global injustice. "What on earth does this little purchase have to do with poverty?" we ask defensively. I slogged and underlined my way through *Consumed*, a remarkable book on the shifting nature of capitalism. After reading most paragraphs twice, the facts settled nicely in the brain space between the "Common Sense" and "Don't Be an Idiot" sections.

Like this obvious commentary:

> Once upon a time, … a productivist capitalism prospered by meeting the real needs of real people. … Today, however, consumerist capitalism profits only when it can address those whose essential needs have already been satisfied but who have the means to assuage "new" and invented needs. … The global majority still has extensive and real natural needs. … But it is without the means to address them, being cut off by the global market's inequality … from the investment in capital and jobs that would allow them to become consumers.[1]

In other words, marketing is used to represent basic needs of humans, without much embellishment. Certainly, the Third World still has these needs in spades—to the detriment of life and health and family—but no consumer power. Thus, Big Marketing turned to the wallet of the privileged, invented a bunch of fake needs (prepackaged sugar water, collagen moisturizer, bleach pens), and disregarded the people who were actually dying every day for lack of basics, exposed to the seductions of the consumer marketplace but without the means to participate in it.

> In this new epoch in which the needy are without income and the wealthy are without needs, radical inequality is simply assumed. … Inequality leaves capitalism with a dilemma: the overproducing capitalist market must either grow or expire. If the poor cannot be enriched enough to become consumers, then grown-ups in the First World who are currently responsible for 60 percent of the world's consumption, and with vast disposable income but few needs, will have to be enticed into shopping.[2]

This is why I had 327 items of clothes in my closet.

With our genuine needs met but so many dollars yet unspent, shopping has become a stronger marker of freedom than voting, and what we spend in the mall matters more than what we're accomplishing together as the church.

I am a part of the problem, a contributing member of inequality. Every time I buy another shirt I don't need or a seventh pair of shoes for my daughter, I redirect my powerful dollar to the pockets of consumerism, fueling my own greed and widening the gap. Why? Because I like it. Because those are cute. Because I want that.

These thoughts burden me holistically, but the trouble is, I can rationalize them individually. This one pair of shoes? Big deal. This little outfit? It was on sale. This microjustification easily translates to nearly every purchase I've made. Alone, each item is reduced to an easy explanation, a harmless transaction. But all together, we've spent enough to irrevocably change the lives of 100,000 people. What did I get for that budgeting displacement? Closets full of clothes we barely wear and enough luxuries to outfit 20 families.

This is hard to process, so it helps to imagine standing in front of the families of my Ethiopian children, who were too poor and sick to raise their own babies. As I gaze upon their hopelessness, I imagine them calculating what I've spent on clothing alone, realizing that same amount would've kept their family fed and healthy for 30 years.

Do you think of your income as a potential source to battle injustice or more like your personal blessing (and reward for working hard)? How does your spending reflect this?

Many factors affect how we evaluate our resources and advantages: the way we were raised, our education level, our immediate communities. Mining your brain, what do your thoughts tell you about your income and privileges?

Plunder

The better question is this: Does God think of our income as a potential source to battle injustice; or is it simply a personal blessing to net us a happy life, a reward for being born in America and not living in a famine and securing an education and solid footing on the economic ladder? ("Objection. Leading the witness." "Objection sustained." "Sorry, Your Honor.")

Throughout the first half of Isaiah, we find the profile of a society under judgment. It's rough waters, man. And while we must study it in the context it was written, only a determined display of denial could ignore the many comparisons to our country today.

God, through Isaiah, made a strong case against Israel. "There is no end to their treasures" (2:7, NIV). Disobedience, slander against Him, the flaunting of sin, greed, idolatry, corruption, arrogance. I've heard of people who struggle with these things, good reader … let us bow our heads and pray for them.

Read Isaiah 3:13–15; an indictment against the "haves" on behalf of the "have-nots." What does God's choice of words and tone of voice tell you about His opinion on these social ills?

This stops me in my tracks: "The plunder from the poor is in your houses" (v. 14). I want to exclude myself from this indictment. I want to believe that filling my house with plunder has nothing to do with the poor, that there is no tenuous thread that connects the two. I don't want to consider myself a privileged vinedresser, commissioned to tend the vine with devotion but devouring it like a wild beast instead. But when God rises up in court as both prosecutor and judge, you *know* you're going to be found guilty.

We enjoy rank and privilege globally; we are the apexes on the pyramid scheme. Acknowledged or not, this position creates an entitlement so entrenched, it is nearly impossible to even imagine we bear responsibility to the poor. Power does this to people subversively; it protects that dangerous blind spot from scrutiny and repentance. Scripture is loaded with dire warnings, which we manage to shove off on other recipients. I mean, we're just talking about clothes here, right? This is a small thing. Harmless.

*Read Isaiah 3:16–4:1. Um. OK. (Isaiah was always known for subtlety.)
The prophet had many vices he could've addressed, but he laid this
one out in striking detail. What link do you see between this outward
description and their inward diseases?*

*Isaiah could've left out verses 18–23 and still kept the accusation intact.
What does the looooong list of clothes and accessories communicate?*

It is so easy to separate ourselves from this description, but if we take a
high view of the industry, couldn't the same paragraph be written about our
fashion obsession today? When one pair of jeans would fund three child sponsorships, and we shop as a habit, and our closets are filled with hundreds and
hundreds of pieces, and we want our kids to look like a Gap ad every day, and
why oh why did Isaiah have to mention "purses" in verse 22? I believe the tail
could indeed be wagging the dog.

God used the following words to describe the women of Judah: haughty, heads
held high, seductive eyes, going along with prancing steps. He painted a
picture of women who want to be seen, even desired. The endless list of superfluous accessories confirmed their vanity. And let's not forget the backdrop
this indictment is issued against: "What do you mean by crushing my people
and grinding the faces of the poor?" (v. 15, NIV). If we read every verse leading
up to these in Isaiah, we find this basic censure: You care about all the wrong
things: religion, not justice for the poor (see 1:11-17); self-advancement, not
orphans and widows (see 1:21-23); wealth, not worship (see 2:7-10); pride, not
humility (see 2:11-18); shameless sin, not repentance (see 3:8-9).

And to this, "the LORD rises to argue the case and stands to judge the people" (v. 13). It's so sobering.

Is it possible you care about some wrong things when it comes to your clothes? Is there any wrong thinking that motivates your purchases? Talk about that.

This discussion is wrought with land mines because we all struggle with defensiveness here. I know I do. I know exactly the arguments: What's wrong with being pretty? I just want to look professional. I want others to take me seriously. I like fashion. How my family dresses is a reflection on me as a provider. I want to look good for my spouse.

Almost all my arguments are rooted in someone else's opinion. Somehow, the exterior dressing is elevated over the content of my character. I imagine that what I am wearing says something more important about me than who I actually am. And evidently I care about that. I cared about it to the tune of 327 pieces of clothing.

Do you have an objection to this discussion? If so, what is it?

Reader, I no more understand your motives here than I do my own sometimes. I am not possibly suggesting I know what makes you tick. I don't know the true reasons that prompt you to put more clothes in your closet, nor am I projecting anything onto you. This is between you and God, and if you're like me, there are umpteen layers to peel back.

Here is my concern: with most of us somewhere in the top 4 percent of earners on earth, we are so far removed from the common human experience, we cannot trust our feelings on this. They will lie to us. Our perspective is tainted with elitism, whether we know it or not. (Simply imagine someone from a developing country walking through our closets; that should do the trick.)

God put it like this in Isaiah 1:5-6:

> "The whole head is hurt, and the whole heart is sick. From the sole of the foot even to the head, no spot is uninjured—wounds, welts, and festering sores not cleansed, bandaged, or soothed with oil."

Is it possible we don't even realize how sick we are? That the same folks walking around pretty and proud are oblivious to our own inner diseases? That underneath the bangles and sashes and perfumes and charms and beauty lays unattended wounds and hearts full of sickness?

If you're thinking, *Lighten up, Jen,* believe me, I want to lighten up. I want to shrug this off as minor. I don't want to be that girl who fusses over how much we spend on clothes and why. I already know some of you are thinking, *I don't like her, I don't like this.* I want you to like me. I want to chill out. I prefer justification to scrutiny here, all day long.

But I can't find any Scripture that will help me. It's like God is serious about this or something. It's as if this particular excess is indicative of heart issues and even deeply connected to injustice. It appears when we secure this specific umbrella of indulgence over our lives, a bunch of serious problems take shelter under there, shielded from examination and restraint and reform.

Maybe it's time to just let it rain.

May I close with some good news from Isaiah? (Yes, there is some.) Read Isaiah 1:18-19,27. There is always a way out with God. Use this space to write your response or maybe a prayer or process your feelings on these Scriptures. Every good turn in our lives starts somewhere small.

Want more? Here are some potential action steps:

- Commit to buying no new clothes, shoes, or accessories for the next month (or six months). See what God does with that extended fast.
- Extend this week by three more. Do a month in those clothes.
- Calculate what you would likely spend on clothes this month, don't buy any, and donate that money to an organization reforming the garment industry or caring for the underresourced who actually need the clothes you can donate.
- For the next six months, put the clothes you wear in a separate section of your closet. Find out how much you actually wear and donate what you do not.
- Have kids? Find an economically disadvantaged school in your community, call the counselor, and ask if the school needs any clothes for students. I bet you have a trunkful to donate.
- Host a "clothing swap" with your friends or neighbors. Have everyone bring any clothes, shoes, and accessories they no longer wear, set up stations, hold up each item and the first responder gets it. Donate the leftovers to a local nonprofit. New-to-you stuff; no money spent.
- Ready to purge all those clothes? Well *hang on* because next week is about to get crazy.

Wrap Up

May I share my clothes fast conclusion from the original 7 project with you?

First, wearing seven clothes was way easier than I expected. In my self-important mind, everyone would notice my repetitions and whisper about my wardrobe. People would obsess about my attire. You know what I discovered? Others aren't thinking about me nearly as much as I thought they were. Blending seamlessly into my environment, I brought up "my clothing situation" 100% more often than it was observed by anyone.

No one really cares. Shockingly, even I don't care as much as I thought. With the boundaries locked in, I lived this month unattached to "looking cute." And no one died. Ministry commenced untainted. Life carried on. I could live my real life on a fraction of my previous wardrobe and nothing significant would be altered. In fact, the simplicity was a blessed relief.

In the grand scheme of things, "how I look to people" all of a sudden just seems ludicrous. Listen, if my influence is linked to my wardrobe, then my ministry is falsely inflated and built on sand. A well-known ministry leader pulled me aside after I received my first multi-book contract and said: "Jen, stay especially connected to Jesus from here on out. With your age and persona, they will try to make a starlet out of you."

At the time, that sounded ridiculous. I was a 29-year-old nobody with a vague notion of my mission. Yet that statement lodged deeply, and I was never able to shake it. In a culture that elevates beauty and style, the Christian community is at genuine risk for distraction, even deception. What do we truly admire in our leaders? Are we no different from the secular population, drawn to charisma and style above substance and integrity?

I hope not.

I want to belong to a Christian community known for a different kind of beauty, the kind that heals and inspires. I can't help but remember Jesus, and how God made sure to mention He was plain and simple by human standards:

"He grew up before Him like a young plant and like a root out of dry ground. He didn't have an impressive form or majesty that we should look at Him, no appearance that we should desire Him. He was despised and rejected by men, a man of suffering who knew what sickness was. He was like someone people turned away from; He was despised, and we didn't value Him" (Isa. 53:2-3).

There was nothing physically attractive about Jesus. He wasn't rich or notorious, well-dressed or handsome. At first glimpse, Jesus was forgettable, neither standing out for beauty or charisma. Maybe this is why the widow and marginalized and sick and outcast flocked to Him. He was approachable in every way.

Jesus didn't garner esteem the conventional way, but make no mistake: He was noticed. He was loved by the outsider, hated by the religious elite, revered by His followers, and killed by His enemies. For a plain carpenter from Nazareth, Jesus sure found His way to the center ring; not through power or ruthlessness but subversion and truth. His humility appeals to the unloveliness in us all. We are drawn in by His simplicity, then transformed by His magnificence.

Oh sure, there will always be people who want Jesus in the Oval Office, on *Primetime*, across from Oprah, on the Red Carpet, spruced up by a stylist and touched up for the cameras. They try to assign Him the power and public sway He always resisted; people want to make a star out of Jesus. But He insisted His power was activated in the margins. Jesus didn't redeem the world on the throne but through the cross.

I don't want to consume the redemption Jesus made possible then spurn the methods by which He achieved it. Jesus' kingdom continues in the same manner it was launched; through humility, subversion, love, sacrifice, through calling empty religion to reform and behaving like we believe the meek will indeed inherit the earth. We cannot carry the gospel to the poor and lowly while emulating the practices of the rich and powerful. We've been invited into a story that begins with humility and ends with glory; never the other way around. Let's align ourselves correctly, sharing in the humble ministry of Jesus, knowing one day we'll feast at His table in splendor.[3]

How did your fast from clothes go this week? What did you learn about yourself? What did you notice about your habits? What was difficult? What was surprising? How did God speak in the empty space? Any breakthroughs? Any disappointments? What will you take away?

Week 4

POSSESSIONS

Video Notes

Group Guide

If a stranger saw your possessions, how would they describe you as the owner? Would their assessment be accurate? Why or why not?

How can you cultivate a sense of God's love in your home?

What can you do differently to be sure possessions don't steer your heart?

Video session downloads available at www.lifeway.com/jenhatmaker

Getting Ready for Possessions

I'm itching to dive into Scripture with you! The Bible is so instructive and wise on this topic. But first things first: Time to nail down your personal fast for the week.

In my one-month version of 7, my family gave away seven things we owned a day. This meant 210 items were headed out the door, but in four weeks, we gave away more like 1,000. I grossly underestimated how much we socked away.

Some were generic donations and others were specific; I tried to look for the perfect recipient. Donating everything through a third party removes the relational magic when one human connects with another. Donating to Goodwill is fine, but about five years ago I read that it's not that rich Christians don't care about the poor; it's that they don't know the poor. It changed my perspective.

This will take some legwork, folks. I spent a good portion of this month driving my stuff somewhere. Purging is one thing; getting it to the right recipient is another. Dig around in your community. Find organizations working with the homeless, the working poor, refugees, underprivileged students, the hungry, single parents, struggling families, and underresourced libraries and schools. Their real needs will be the engine behind your choices.

After purging over 200 items from my closet alone (true story), we decided to limit "clothes giveaways" to just one week, even though the numbers far exceeded our original intent. In this format, you would hit the target number if you purged just 49 items of clothes, so perhaps you'd like to take a similar approach and dedicate one or two days for purging clothes. With our closets burgeoning, including spouses and kids, it's just too easy.

This was the first month our kids joined the experiment. We gave them full reign over their own things, and they were far more generous than we would've been on their behalf. We donated most of their clothes to one of our city's poorest schools; the counselor was thrilled. Their toys and games went to a children's shelter.

As always, if you are a parent, engage your children however you see fit. Our families are all different and our kids are in different places, so you include them in whatever way works for you.

Here are some other options for this week:

- I highly recommend doing at least part of this week in community, like I did. (If you're studying this in a small group, voila.) What you and your friends can do together is incredible.
- Each family member can purge seven items a day for the week.
- Want to hit the same target number as if this was a month instead of a week? Purge 30 items each day. Total: 210.
- Give away at least seven items from every room and closet in the house.
- Choose seven categories to purge (clothes, toys, kitchen goods, linens, home accessories, furniture, etc.) and dedicate one day to each.
- Give away seven things in seven categories per person.
- Choose seven organizations in your community to donate your things to.
- For big ticket items, sell them online and donate the proceeds. (One 7 reader downsized from her four-bedroom home into an apartment, sold over half her belongings, and single-handedly funded a safe house in Haiti. Junk into justice.)
- Do you have piles of stuff stored in a shed? Attic? Storage unit? Garage? Use this week to heavily purge, reduce, or eliminate these dedicated spaces that simply contain your extra stuff.

After discussing with your spouse, family, roommates, or partners in crime, how have you decided to fast from possessions this week?

What are your concerns?

Jesus Dishes on Economics

My oldest son, Gavin, recently asked me, "Mom? What do you think is one of the top burning questions in life?"

I answered, "Oh, maybe *why do really bad things happen to really good people?*"

To which he replied, "No, Mom, real life stuff, like *can you cry underwater* or *why don't birds get electrocuted when they land on telephone lines?*"

Oh, I see. *Real* life stuff. Pardon me.

This week, I will be playing the role of Jen Hatmaker, student/writer of Bible things who digs deep, thrashes around, struggles mightily with the content, *mightily*, and writes stuff down anyway. For me, one of the burning questions in life for Western believers is this: How do we manage our wealth, financial priorities, and possessions with godliness and integrity?

Good reader, I do not have this subject figured out, much less mastered. I am with you, side by side on this difficult material. So may we wrestle through Scripture with much grace for one another this week, just brothers and sisters trying to figure out this Christian life.

I've said often that if I had to tear one page out of the Bible and it's all I got, I'd choose the Sermon on the Mount. It's Jesus out there on the radical twig of the radical limb of the radical branch of Christianity (or as Jesus called it: ordinary discipleship). It is, plain and simple, the believer's manifesto for living. To me, this passage is Jesus at His finest, making exactly zero people comfortable and basically blowing everyone's minds for the rest of time.

Read Matthew 6:19–21. Jesus didn't use emotionalism here, but logic. Imagine Him taking us firmly by the shoulders and driving His point home: What do you hear Jesus saying?

Roughly 15 percent of Jesus' recorded teachings relate to this topic, more than those about heaven and hell combined.[1] Jesus was simply relentless in His call toward lean living and reckless generosity. He never let up, refused to soften the blow of it all. Then He busted out the worst weapon ever: reasonableness.

Jesus gave us some clues in this teaching to expose any wrong thinking we may feed. First, He uncovered a fundamental correlation between our spiritual health and how we think about and handle money. These aren't two separate things. They aren't two unrelated drawers in our spiritual dresser. They are so tightly linked, in fact, that Jesus basically said, "Show me how you spend your money, and I'll show you what you really love." Jesus didn't say our hearts would predicate our treasures, but that *our treasures would steer our hearts.* These treasures … they have serious power. Evidently, the hoarding of possessions induces an inordinate love for them.

Identify the treasure, find the heart. In general, what do our houses jammed with possessions seem to indicate about what we treasure?

If "stored earthly treasures" is a clue about your spiritual health like Jesus suggested, what do you see? Any red flags signaling some wrong thinking? (Check your reaction to this passage and discussion as a hint.)

It might be helpful to unpack the term "treasures." In this context, Jesus clearly denoted material possessions. In fact, He told a little story about our favorite things to amass, and here is the last chapter: infested —> corroded —> stolen. The most unhappy ending ever. Jesus had the advantage of eternal perspective that is *just so stinking hard to grasp.* He never said these possessions were bad; He said they wouldn't last. And like a wise parent, Jesus asks us: "Why would you spend so much time and energy and money on things that won't last? Why would you do that?" Wrong thinking, that's why.

Following that trail, if we mistakenly spend the majority of this short life on earth earning more, buying bigger, possessing nicer, and chasing better, then at the end we have this: a mostly wasted life. Jesus begged us not to get trapped in materialism, because not only does it derail our purpose here, it's stupid. Our stuff will matter for zero seconds after we die, and all it does is steal precious time, energy, and resources away from our true mission here.

The "Eyes" Have It

If we think of treasures as "what we derive our happiness from," that helps us get a little closer to the bulls-eye. Again, Jesus made this easier by creating two camps of potential happiness: earthly treasures or heavenly treasures. This is really where we winnow the chaff. This is a piercing question. What really makes you happy?

In context, we have these happiness options: a beautiful home, gorgeous furnishings, lots of accessories and gadgets, sweet cars, the latest fashions, big savings accounts, stuff, things, luxuries. Conversely, we have these happiness options: generosity, living below our means, giving, intentional restraint, battling poverty, simplicity, sharing, communal responsibility, humility.

Infuriatingly, Jesus didn't offer a middle ground. Which happiness pool do you mostly swim in? Jesus told us to check our bank statements and what we think about most if we aren't sure. If you are conflicted, talk about that.

This entire sermon is pragmatic, truthful, reasonable. With precision, Jesus told us the best way to live. The end. These principles, counterintuitive as they seem, lead to freedom. Jesus never steered us wrong. He never embellished or glossed over difficult ideas. He didn't use weird words or try to trick us. But He did say often that only those with ears to hear and eyes to see could ever receive His policies.

So when I read this passage and my heart bucks, defensiveness rises up, and I start angling for loopholes, this tells me I entertain some wrong thinking, because it conflicts with Jesus' ideas which are always true, always right, always best. I want to invent a shade of gray here or navigate the fictitious middle ground, but anytime I'm at odds with Jesus, I am on the losing end of the debate. Maybe I need to check my ears and eyes.

Read Matthew 6:22–23. Why do you think Jesus followed up verses 19–21 with these words? What do you think He was suggesting?

We must assume these verses had something to do with the ones that preceded and followed them, even though they sound disconnected. It is helpful to peek at the original language, which offers interesting insight into Jesus' choice of words.

Most of our translations say, "If your eye is *good* ..." Often in the translation between two languages, intent is lost. I mean, what is *good*? Homemade salsa is good. Sunday naps are good. Football season is good. My son Caleb pretends to be good. Good means too many things for us.

The closer meaning to the Greek word used, *haplous*, is "clear, single, simple." One thing I loooooove about Scripture is how many layers of truth it manages to contain. And Jesus was especially skilled at layering depth upon depth with a clever turn of phrase or a brilliant use of metaphor.

If you inserted "clear, single, simple" for "good" in verse 22, keeping the materialism context intact, how does that change your interpretation of this sentence? What might Jesus be driving at?

Possessions

What are the dangers of operating with double vision literally?

As it relates to materialism, what are the dangers of operating with double vision spiritually?

That simple lexicon seriously helps connect these sections, but there is even more. Jesus was not using this word carelessly. Words closely related to haplous mean "liberality" and "generously." We see this meaning in Romans 12:8 when Paul wrote that God gifts some with special generosity, and again in 2 Corinthians 9:11 when Paul commended the cheerful giver and promised that God would reward his openhandedness, and in James 1:5 where God is praised for His generous dispersion of wisdom.

If your eyes are *generous* …

Bookmark that, and let's switch to the other word: "bad." What is bad, folks? Brussel sprouts are bad. Gossip is bad. The end of football season is bad. Joan Jett is bad (to the bone). Bad means too many things to us, too.

"Bad" is from the word *poneros*, usually meaning *evil*, but it is also used in translating the Hebrew expression "evil eye," a Jewish colloquialism meaning *grudging* or *stingy*. It is—once again—wrapped up in the concept of money and possessions. We find it in certain translations, like in Deuteronomy 15:9, where God instructs His people to loan generously to the destitute, lest "your *eye is hostile* toward your poor brother" (NASB, emphasis added) and also in Proverbs 28:22 which says, "A man with an *evil eye* hastens after wealth" (NASB, emphasis added).

The Evil Eye

We find a helpful parallel in the parable of the workers in the vineyard in Matthew 20:1-16, although it is mangled in translation. As the story goes, the landowner went out early to hire day workers and agreed to pay them a denarius for the day. He hired some in the morning, some at midday, others in the afternoon, and a few with only an hour left in the workday. At the close of business, he paid every worker one denarius, whether they started at 6:00 a.m. or 5:00 p.m. The early morning workers were furious, feeling cheated, and made a big stink.

The landowner asked in verse 15 (in most our translations): "Don't I have the right to do what I want with my business? Are you jealous because I'm generous?" which is a fine paraphrase, but a translation closer to the original Greek reads: "Or is your eye evil because I am good?" (NKJV).

So here we have this "bad eye" thing again, and it is related to a hostile reaction to generosity. Jesus was describing a bad eye as one that could not see the beauty of grace, the brightness of benevolence. It focused too intently on the wrong part of the story. It interpreted money and material reward as more desirable than openhanded goodness and free, gracious, God-like liberality. It was a bad eye, man.

The layers keep piling up, making a real case against greed, for generosity.

Take some of the above words and definitions and ideas and supporting Scriptures, and rewrite Matthew 6:22-23, expanding or adding or paraphrasing or compiling several ideas into one.

This warning has an upside. If we manage to fall on the right side of this argument, "your whole body will be full of light" (v. 22). Jesus seemed to say that if our heart, represented by our eye, is generous, then our entire spiritual life will be flooded with brightness. Dark corners banished. Obscured areas bathed in light. Our path illuminated. Our purpose clear in the light of day. Our hearts released from the oppressive, black trappings that threaten to plunge us into darkness. The heavy cloak of worry, anxiety, and fear that surrounds accumulation lifted.

Good readers, I wish I could insert my experiences from this month of 7 here because they were so rich, but let me simply tell you what I learned viscerally: The more openhanded I became with my stuff, the less power they had over me. A brightness truly began flooding some dark recesses of my heart, ugly places where I wanted to protect my things, shelter my safety net, and harbor my justifications. It was like magic.

Jesus was right. Our hearts *are* deeply connected to our treasures, and the more I gave away, the less I considered them treasures at all. I couldn't talk myself into feeling differently. I couldn't talk myself out of wanting more. I just had to give them away, and therein was the miracle. "We don't think our way into a new life; we live our way into a new kind of thinking."[2] Maybe this is one of those truths that must be lived to learn.

Have you ever discovered this upside-down truth in giving away? The lightness and brightness of it all? Tell your story.

We'd be remiss to skip over Jesus' warning: "If your eye is bad, your whole body will be full of darkness. So if the light within you is darkness—how deep is that darkness!" (v. 23). This petrifies me, this observation. Possessions, greed, stuff … it has the power to lie to me, to help me lie to myself, to help me believe my lying self.

My own bad eye will trick me. It will say, "This darkness? This? In your heart and life? This insatiable wanting and cavalier squandering of resources? No, no. *That's light.* This stuff is where the light comes from! Get more! Obsess about it! Then you'll have even more light! Look around. The flash and sparkle, the glitz and glam, the pop; this is where happiness comes from, man."

If the light within me is actually darkness, oh how deep that darkness is.

That darkness is a liar, masquerading as light—the worst kind. It feels so believable. Sure, we have plenty of people at the tip top of the food chain who confess their stuff didn't bring the joy, didn't fill the empty space, didn't work like they thought it would. They admit money didn't actually buy happiness; the system lied. But we think, *well, just let me get to that level and I'll test the theory myself, thank you very much.*

Darkness is never more dangerous than when we're plunged in it and think we can see. The financial decisions we make are wrought with peril. Our justifications are full of holes we can't make out. How we raise our children, run our churches, consider our communities, interpret who our neighbor is—when done in false illumination, we can sink an entire society, mislead a generation, abandon billions in their suffering, misinterpret the scope of the gospel.

The bad eye is so scary.

In your opinion, what are some of the worst lies the bad eye convinces us to believe when it comes to money and possessions? As families? As churches? (Loaded question alert.)

Who's Your Daddy?

So Jesus has clearly not gone off topic as it may have sounded. Somehow, He managed to power pack these 10 sentences with so much depth, we can mine new truths indefinitely. He wrapped up the tutorial like this.

Read Matthew 6:24. Jesus set "money" up as a competing master to His own reign in our lives. He refuted the common perception that it is possible for us to seek both. What does Jesus seem to know about the human heart?

Jesus completed the flow chart of materialism:

treasures —> heart —> self-deception —> enslavement

I'd prefer His final argument ended with "distracted" rather than "enslaved," but noooo. It starts with earthly treasures, which begets misplaced affection/allegiance, which then requires some spiritual two-stepping, and it inevitably ends, not with owning more, but by being owned.

There is a practical side to Jesus' argument, as always. A man may serve two masters in succession, even if the first is utterly unlike the second. He may serve two masters with opposite character; one in appearance only and the other in reality. A man may serve two masters unequally, doing random acts of service to one while habitually, faithfully, consistently serving the other. He may serve two masters on the same side, like serving his Commander in Chief as well as his direct officer, as they support the same objective and obeying one means obeying the other. But no man can be at the same time, in reality, a loyal servant of two masters hostile to each other, whose interests stand in diametric opposition.

If he thinks he is pulling it off, he is self-deceived, says Jesus, because it is impossible.

We can, we say, we're doing it now.

You can't, says Jesus, your light is actually darkness.

God, money ... these are very powerful masters, both tending to induce complete subjection. These are not trite forces to be dealt with casually. Just as God is not "our buddy" indulging our whims and content with semi-allegiance, neither is money a benign, harmless line item we can safely disregard. These masters will take our all, demand our full loyalty. There is no middle ground with either, although one is truthful about His expectations and the other is a liar. We can only be slaves to one, not both. Here is why.

As masters, they want completely opposite things.

For each godly directive below, what does the Money Master substitute?

Be humble. _____

Set your affections on kingdom things. _____

Don't worry about possessions. _____

Be grateful. _____

Be obscenely generous. _____

Embrace your responsibility to the poor. _____

Spend your energy on kingdom work. _____

Love your neighbor. _____

Live simply (the good eye). _____

These masters simply cannot coach the same team. We cannot be obedient to the mandates on the left while still clamoring for those on the right. *We just can't.* One master will slowly pull us away from the other, bit by bit, for righteousness or for self-destruction. Eventually, we will be devoted to one and despise the other.

This is another helpful clue as we diagnose our own spiritual condition: *What do we despise more?* Do we hate the power money exerts over us? Do we make intentional financial choices that break the materialism chains? Do we hate poverty and offer our lives as a remedy? Do we hate the gross abuses money inspires in mankind? Do we hate the whispers of greed and entitlement we see in our children, mirror images of our own affections? Do we hate the comparison game money feeds off of? Do we hate the inequity that gives our kids rooms jammed with possessions while 16,000 other parents will bury their starved children today?

Or do we hate this discussion? Do we hate these questions? Would we rather spin this or twist this or shove this off on other people? Do we hate being challenged to care for the poor, since they didn't earn this money we worked for? Do we hate Jesus and God and Jen Hatmaker snooping around our bank accounts, claiming they can discern all there is to know by the line items? (I hate how God uses me against myself. That's so sneaky.) Do we hate the idea of parting with things? Do we hate the implication that rich people are predisposed to the bad eye? Do we hate being called "rich people"?

Which do you despise more? How did you answer some of these questions?

Now the big question: What do we do with all this? Do we sell everything we own and give our money away indiscriminately? Do we downsize, share rooms, give away extra cars, and free up half our budget to disperse? Do we never buy anything again? Do we hack up our savings account and share it with refugees? Do we all move to Africa? We need answers. We need to know. Someone tell us what to do.

Because Jesus gave us two distinct camps—opposites, enemies, rivals—we'd like the nice, neat, easily delineated Life Story to match. It would be so fabulous to say, "Yes! I am all this and never that! I've chosen correctly! I'm in the right category always!" Or if we find ourselves serving the wrong master, it's tempting to despair here, throw our hands in the air, imagining these things will own us forever.

But here is the truth: This side of heaven, we will never find ourselves on the right side of the kingdom all the time. I won't. You won't. Rather than assessing this area as one sum total, already determined, imagine this part of discipleship as a thousand little moments, thousands of small decisions that bit by bit, choice by choice, slowly draw us under the leadership of the correct Master.

When you purge your closets and give to a struggling family ... that counts.

When you skip those new shoes and sponsor a child with that money ... that counts.

When you help fund your friend's adoption in some small way ... that counts.

When you spend more energy on people than decorating ... that counts.

When you give, share, contribute, provide for someone else ... that counts.

Every day, we have incremental chances to store up heavenly treasures, to foster good eyes, to be filled with light, to serve and love our God and His people. None of these alone will define us; individually, these moments won't draw a line in the sand declaring, "This. This is the day it all came together." Nor will any of them alone disqualify us from this conversation or seal our fate as Money Slaves.

But together, the dots start connecting in a certain direction. Each small decision connects to the next and slowly forms a new pathway. The clues start to work in our favor. They begin revealing a heart that loves people more than possessions, justice more than a huge savings account. They may even tap us on the shoulder one day and say, "Hey, guess what? You haven't bought new clothes in over a year." The clues may show us things we despise, and lo and behold, they are the same things God despises this time. Something is happening. It started with habits and ended with our hearts; God did that somehow. I guess Jesus was right:

"Where your treasure is, there your heart will be also." Matthew 6:21

The only way to eat an elephant is one bite at a time. Can you think of five simple choices you can make that will draw you closer to the right treasures, and in doing so, help put distance between you and the wrong ones? Pray about it. God is so for you in this department. He wants this for us.

Want More?

Consider these options (and others) mentioned at the beginning of the week to do in community:

- Furnish an apartment for a refugee family or transitioning family. Make some calls and volunteer. This is easier than you think.
- Pool your purged items, throw a massive garage sale, and do something extraordinary with the proceeds. (My readers and I are building our fifth safe house for at-risk kids in Haiti with our collective garage sale profits. You could build one too: *www.garagesale4orphans.org.*)

- Secure a storage space (spare room at your church, repurposed room in someone's home, reclaimed garage) and organize a donation center with your friends. Pool your items (clothes, kitchen goods, toiletries, bedding, linens, accessories, appliances, etc.) and organize them for quick dispersion. Contact your churches and local relief organizations and let them know you have items ready to deliver.

And here are a few more to think about:

- Commit to purchasing no more _____ (fill in the blank with your vice) for the next year.
- Organize a Hand-Me-Down group for your kids with diverse-sized participants, and commit to receiving and passing on clothes and shoes for the next season instead of buying all new.
- Have an extra car? Anyone need it more than you? Could you change someone's life with it? (Many single parents without cars are in a desperate spot.)

- On the cusp of radical? Consider purging and downsizing.
- Our homes are our largest assets. Want to use it for the kingdom more? Consider adopting or fostering; taking in a family or person in transition or need; or starting a Book Club, Supper Club, Game Night, Weekly Brunch, anything open to neighbors and friends not connected to Jesus.

Wrap Up

Here's my original wrap up, ironically including the same Scriptures we studied:

> After a month of liquidating, my friends and I still have stuff to give away. I am not even kidding. Our closets, drawers, cabinets, garages, attics, and shelves have been purged, and the volume created a pit in my stomach I can't shake.
>
> When did this lose relevance for me?
>
> "Don't collect for yourselves treasures on earth, where moth and rust destroy and where thieves break in and steal. But collect for yourselves treasures in heaven, where neither moth nor rust destroys, and where thieves don't break in and steal. For where your treasure is, there your heart will be also" (Matt. 6:19-21).
>
> There is no middle road. ... Grayed-down discipleship is an easier sell, but it created pretend Christians, obsessing over Scriptures we like while conspicuously ignoring the rest. Until God asks for everything and we answer, "It's Yours," we don't yet have ears to hear or eyes to see. We're still deaf to the truth, blind to freedom, deceived by the treasures of the world, imagining them to be the key when they are actually the lock.
>
> Nothing like handing over a big pile of your stuff to drive this point home! ... But now here's the real issue: Will I just replace all this? Will I purge another 1000 items three years from now? Will I slowly refill the empty spaces? Or will my family disconnect from the machine, creating a more courageous legacy than simply consuming? I want to confront the big part that says "more" with the smaller part that says "enough."
>
> Believers, let's oppose the powers that manipulate us, lying about our needs, our responsibilities, our neighbor. ... But be prepared for the upstream struggle. The keepers of the market want us to spend. In a typical year, the United States spends about $16 billion in foreign aid, and $276 billion on advertising.
>
> Paul put it this way: "When I was a child, I talked like a child, I thought like a child, I reasoned like a child. When I became a

man, I put the ways of childhood behind me. For now we see only a reflection as in a mirror; then we shall see face to face. Now I know in part; then I shall know fully, even as I am fully known" (1 Cor. 13:11-12).

A child says "me." An adult says "us." Maturity deciphers need from want, wisdom from foolishness. Growing up means curbing appetites, shifting from "me" to "we," understanding private choices have social consequences and public outcomes. Let's be consumers who silence the screaming voice that yells, "I WANT!" and instead listens to the quiet "we need," the marginalized voice of the worldwide community we belong to.

We top the global food chain through no fault or credit of our own. I've asked God a billion times why I have so much while others have so little. Why do my kids get full bellies? Why does water flow freely from my faucets? Why do we get to go the doctor when we're sick? There is no easy answer. The "why" definitely matters, but so does the "what." What do we do with our riches? What do we do with our privileges? What should we keep? What should we share? I better address this inequality since Jesus clearly identified the poor as His brothers and sisters and my neighbor.

What if we tried together? What if a bunch of Christians wrote a new story, becoming consumers the earth is groaning for? I suspect we'd find that elusive contentment, storing up treasures in heaven like Jesus told us to. I'm betting our stuff would lose its grip and we'd discover riches contained in a simpler life, a communal responsibility. *Money* is the most frequent theme in Scripture; perhaps the secret to happiness is right under our noses. Maybe we don't recognize satisfaction because it is disguised as radical generosity, a strange misnomer in a consumer culture.

"We're just about to become adults, to honestly let the Gospel speak to us, to listen to what Jesus says, … about poverty and about leading a simple life in this world, a life that shows trust in God and not in our own power. … God never promised us security in this world. God promised us only truth and freedom in our hearts. … What does all this mean for us? It means that we're on the way."[3]

Let's prove that theory correct.[4]

How did your fast from possessions go this week? What did you learn about yourself? What did you notice about your habits? What was difficult? What was surprising? How did God speak in the empty space? Any breakthroughs? Any disappointments? What will you take away?

Video Notes

Group Guide

How plugged in do you think you are? Would your family and friends agree or disagree with your answer? Why?

How has being plugged in distracted you from real-life relationships?

How can you redirect your media and technology time into time invested in relationships?

How can you develop real-life relationships as a "sent" follower of Christ? What's one way you can better represent Christ in your community?

Video session downloads available at *www.lifeway.com/jenhatmaker*

Getting Ready for Media

What, oh, what are we ever going to study in the Bible about media and technology? ("Jesus then said, 'Come, follow Me … on Twitter'" [Nowhere 6:18].) Don't worry, good reader, we have much to glean from our ancient text on this modern issue. But let's nail down your personal fast this week first.

In the original experiment, our family shut down seven screens.

TV   Gaming

Facebook, Twitter, & Social Media

iPhone apps   Radio

Texting*   Internet**

*This one involved much discussion. Texting is a double-edged sword. Sometimes it is a time saver, and other times it is extraneous, even ridiculous. So our texting rule was: If it was a time saver and/or necessary, then text away. If it was to be sarcastic, silly, or inappropriate, then pass.

**The Internet was a necessary tool for our jobs and life. Brandon and I couldn't ditch it for a month because of the boring stuff: work, correspondence, research, writing. We did leave behind the fun stuff like *Sportcenter.com, StuffChristiansLike.net,* Hulu, *scanwiches.com,thepioneerwoman.com,* and YouTube. Good-bye.

For most of us, this will take a bit of prep. Inform your people that you will be off Facebook, off Twitter, only checking urgent e-mails, not texting, or whatever limits you've chosen. If folks are accustomed to having instant access to you, declaring your boundaries is helpful for everyone.

Parents, this is a whole family endeavor, unless you plan on locking yourself in the closet while your kids watch TV and Facebook their friends. But again, depending on your children's ages and stages, this will look different for all of us. You choose media and technology limits that make sense for your family. There is no one-size-fits-all here.

Feel free to shut down the whole circus, or here are some alternatives to try:

- Dedicate only one hour a day to any media or technology this week.
- Let each family member pick only one screen option for the week and only for a limited time. (Gaming for 30 minutes a day, one TV show, Facebook for 15 minutes a day, etc.)
- Choose a cut-off time in which every family member turns in phones, laptops, and games each day.
- Make a media-alternative plan for each day/night: Family Game Night, picnic in the backyard, bike to the park, go to a free museum, invite another family over, take a family walk/hike, Kids Make Dinner Night, serve someone … you get the idea.
- Choose one day of the week for media and technology time, and go cold turkey on the other six days.
- Perhaps it isn't *how much you watch*, but *what you watch* you'd like to address. Decide with your family which shows or Web sites or apps or games to eliminate.
- Choose seven people to connect with this week in place of media consumption.
- Declare screen-free zones: dining table, bedrooms, car, family room. Maybe include a screen-free segment of the day as another zone.
- Dedicate seven consecutive hours a day to no screens.

After discussing with your spouse, family, roommates, or partners in crime, how have you decided to fast from media and technology this week?

What are your concerns?

Darla Star

In 1990, when I was a sophomore in high school, my friend Steve started bringing reams of printouts to school. Evidently he and his techie friends stumbled on this "Internet technology" and were "connecting" via "typed messages" to strangers, printing out their dialogue for our entertainment. (Online, he and his friends pretended to be a 25-year-old named Darla Star, a product of the collective brainpower of four 15-year-olds, but that is neither here nor there.)

The rest of us were perplexed by this communiqué: How do you send the message? How do you find someone to send it to? Do you have to be a member of "the Internet"? Are there fees? Is it for real people or just liars like you? Do we need to know how to program? Why would someone type a message when they could just call? Like people are all going to have home computers! We're not millionaires.

Flash forward to today: I cannot be unplugged for three hours without someone demanding, *"Where are you? I've e-mailed you through both addresses and sent you two Tweets and three texts. Why are you screening me?!"* My time no longer belongs to me, and if I disconnect for a few hours, people take it as a personal affront. Sometimes I miss the days when the Internet was simply an outlet for techie sophomore boys and their imaginations.

Add television. DVR. Tivo. Movies on Demand. Primetime on Demand. Kids on Demand. Pay-Per-View Sports Package. Texting. Phone apps. Facebook. Twitter. One zillion blogs. Pandora. iTunes. Sirius XM. Pinterest. YouTube. Wii. Xbox. Nintendo 360. Apple TV. Netflix. LinkedIn. (Just kidding! No one is on that.) Every Web site for every idea for everything on earth. It's a wonder our brains have not turned to straight porridge.

The Bible may not have anything to say about Google+, but it has plenty to say about what we look at, how we discern truth from lies, how we spend our time, and how to foster (or sabotage) real community.

Read John 17:15-18. What is Jesus' policy on our place on earth as His followers? Describe every principle you see.

I grew up in a Christian culture that valued a sequestered worldview. "In the world, not of the world" was the mantra that kept me separated from "sinners," isolated from complicated questions, and quarantined with other believers. Doubt made me uncomfortable. Messy issues boggled my theology. A heavy emphasis on morality reduced my concept of discipleship into simple lists; do this and be esteemed, do that and be condemned.

I artfully skipped over the part where Jesus said, "I am not praying that You take them out of the world. … As You sent Me into the world, I also have sent them into the world." I avoided this concept, preferring a protectionist view-point, meaning pull out, detach, ignore, disengage, disconnect, wall it off. My answer was to live in a Christian bunker where none of it could reach me and mine. Problem solved.

But Jesus chose a different way to protect us: truth. Evidently, He deemed *that* enough to anchor us; severance was apparently unnecessary. Armed with truth, we can live in this world with great purpose, extreme effective-ness, boundless hope. Truth is the linchpin, protecting both our holiness and usefulness.

Snakes and Doves

The pursuit of biblical truth is the key to this week's discussion. Let's set the cultural stage, addressing media we simply consume first (TV, movies, music, print media), and we'll deal with social media next. The media is one that, well, mediates, conveying the knowledge, truth, ideas, feelings, perspectives, and ideologies of those who have access to it.

Obviously, this is not an "all bad" scenario. Media can be productive, instruc-tive, harmlessly entertaining, and mobilizing. Absolutely it can. I love certain shows and movies and music for the same reasons I love books: fascinating stories, unforgettable characters, life portrayed, creative expression. This is no rant to throw it out but rather to practice evaluation by discerning motives, tactics, inherent messages, marketing maneuvers, and harmful objectives.

For most of society, the mass media provides the content from which we develop our sense of self, the nature of our relationships, our view of the world, and our deepest values and concerns. Ironically, those who are most affected by U.S. popular culture are those who pay the least attention to its influence.

Peter Greenaway of Deakin University in Australia suggested that in order for one to understand a culture, one must "go outside of it" and that Americans seldom do that.[1]

Considering mainstream media ideologies, how would you generally describe the message conveyed for each of the following?

Money _____

Sex _____

Power _____

Violence _____

Body image _____

Life purpose _____

Faith _____

How do you see discrepancies between mainstream media and the truth Christ calls us to live out as His followers?

This is where my old mantra was helpful; categorize, demonize, and avoid. Tra la la. But as Jesus insisted on sending us into this world, perhaps there is a strategy superior to pretending none of it exists. Maybe remaining culturally savvy, sharp, and discerning, shrewd as snakes and innocent as doves is an advantage.

When asked about takeaways from 7, one permanent change was this: I developed sharper critical thinking when it came to media ideologies and its sugar daddy, advertising. My sense of hearing became acute, and I could discern the tiniest whispers of deception, often undetected before. My media literacy increased, which is more useful than, say, ignorance.

With the media cultivating popular groupthink on issues like hate/love, stereotyping, violence, sexual norms, wealth, religion, and personal identity, we would be foolish to stick our heads in the sand, because how can we offer an alternative if we don't understand the archetype? Either sequestering renders us unapproachable, unable to connect, and impotent as knowledgeable, attentive Christ-followers here on a mission, or careless ignorance of our own media consumption replaces truth with lies in our minds and in our children's minds while we drink the Kool-Aid to our great detriment.

If 1 is "absolutely no media, circa 1874" and 10 is "plugged in all day, little discernment," where do you and your family fall?

1   2   3   4   5   6   7   8   9   10

Do you strike a healthy balance, or does media consumption cause you tension? Talk about that.

In John 17:17, Jesus prayed, "Sanctify them by the truth; Your word is truth." This is how Jesus prayed for our protection: knowing His Word, an instrument of discernment. In this specific discussion, truth recognizes the information leveled at us is an expression of the ideas, values, and ideologies of the source, which requires careful scrutiny. Through biblical truth, we develop the ability to sift through and analyze the messages that inform, entertain, and sell to us every day.

Truth is why I hear this local radio commercial on home furnishings—"*We'll get you everything you need. Oh, who are we kidding? We'll get you everything you want!*"— and cringe at the lie it perpetuates, assuring us we deserve more, better, bigger, and can shrug that impulse off with a casual wave and clever aside.

Truth is why I pulled up programming *aimed at children* wrought with high school sex, lies, betrayals, and rebellion and talked my two middle school kids through it. We discussed how characters were reduced and stereotyped, consequences were trivialized, and the views became normative and socializing.

Truth is the reason I analyzed a teen magazine with my sixth-grade daughter. We picked apart the ads, identifying marketing tactics that preyed on her insecurities, promising results hair spray could never actually deliver. I asked her: What do they know about teenage girls that they are exploiting to sell their product? What are the images and words designed to make you feel? Truth helped her realize marketers want her brand loyalty, her heart, and her money (ditto: *all of us*).

Truth is the reason we enjoy certain shows and movies together, no problem.

Truth protects our identities from the popular media qualifiers of power, position, possessions, and beauty.

Truth turns us into wise teachers, not simply avoiders.

Truth helps us embrace the good elements of media and resist the bad, for it contains both.

This one may sting a bit, so brace yourself. How much time do you spend absorbing biblical truth compared to absorbing media? Talk about it.

Christian Fighting

We are not the first believers surrounded by destructive messages. The early church, absolute minorities in culture, constantly had to check their intake and rage against the machine.

Read 2 Corinthians 10:2-5. List everything Paul said our weapons could demolish.

How does your media intake affect your thoughts?

If media can capture our thoughts, it can capture our hearts and minds and wallets. (Remember Matthew 6:21 from possessions week?) *This stuff really matters.* This session caused me much anxiety because I don't want it boiled down to a morality issue. That is too easy. That is the safe argument. Claiming high moral ground on issues is exactly the kind of stuff Jesus told us we'd get hung up on while missing the greater offenders, straining out gnats and gulping down camels.

I'm more concerned about the casual portrayal of wealth, the top priorities of self-indulgence and gratification, the toxic depiction of marriage, the definition of success, the parroting of the American Dream, the endless enticements to buy more, want more, have more, and how this constant intake affects us. These infiltrate our thoughts, depicting a "normal" that renders our entire Bible obsolete. Think seeing someone smoke on TV is insidious? Try watching an absent dad spend 800K on a sweet 16 birthday party for his entitled, self-obsessed daughter with Lil' Bow Wow flown in to deejay. (Jesus, come quickly.)

I realize just because we see shameless affairs in movies doesn't mean we're going to have one. Watching families self-destruct on reality shows doesn't mean ours will implode. Seeing constant renovation projects on Pinterest doesn't mean we're going to take out a second mortgage to achieve the same.

Hearing racial stereotypes reinforced in music doesn't mean we will turn into bigots. Every kid who plays Halo won't morph into the alien Arbiter in a 26th-century conflict between the human United Nations Space Command and genocidal Covenant.

But does that mean these are all good for us? Also to the Corinthians, Paul wrote: " 'Everything is permissible,' but not everything is helpful. 'Everything is permissible,' but not everything builds up" (1 Cor. 10:23). I can no more decide what this looks like for you than figure out my Apple TV. This is no place to compare or judge. We assess beauty and struggle and creativity and stories differently. Some messages roll off you like Teflon, but they lodge in my thoughts for days. Others don't affect me in the slightest, but they plant ideas in your head you can't shake. And still others are probably a bad idea for all of us. Just because we can, doesn't mean we should.

Think about the shows, movies, games, and print media you and your family consume. Evaluate them below, keeping in mind Paul's words.

Is it less a content issue and more a quantity issue in your home? Media = time. Thoughts?

Would you consider any of the above as "strongholds" that need to be demolished (either content or quantity)? If so, what is the power they hold over you?

Friending, Pinning, and Other New Verbs

Let's now skip over to Facebook, shall we? And don't panic, I shan't be calling for a boycott of social media, for the love of the land. How else would I know that someone's "big boy went pee-pee on the big boy potty today"? This is important information and I need it in my gray matter. (Roll eyes here.)

This is new territory for us. Social media is so fresh on the scene; we've barely set our passwords, much less ferreted its impact and discerned long-term effects. I've been on Facebook for three years and Twitter for ten months. But since the disciples only had three years with Jesus then proceeded to *spread the gospel to the ends of the earth*, I guess I can write two thousand words about updating our statuses.

Social media has not just given us a new way to connect, it has given us a new set of verbs: Facebooking, tweeting, retweeting, pinning, repinning, posting, *liking*, friending, unfriending (sorry, oversharers), texting, screening, linking, procrastinating (that last one was mine). We have all these new things to do now that didn't even exist eight years ago.

Let's start with the good news: What positive effects do you see with the advent of social media?

Social media has some wonderful, even remarkable upshots. It shrunk the world. I've made relational connections online—some old, some new—that have altered my path for good forever. Together, my Facebook and Twitter friends built six safe houses for aged-out orphaned girls in Haiti, entirely accomplished through social media. I've engaged nuanced issues with smart, engaged readers, on my blog and others, elevating civil discourse and sharpening one another. Social media helps raise money, raise awareness, raise community, and raise children.

Let's call social media neutral: could be awesome, could be terrible, depending on how we handle it. If we take the "truth" approach we discussed earlier, then we need not stage a boycott, but rather thoughtfully engage without checking our brains at the door.

Proverbs may be ancient, but wisdom and truth pay forward indefinitely. Perhaps Solomon didn't say, "A fool posts before thinking, but a wise man walks away from his aunt's political rant on Facebook," but he gave us plenty of wisdom as we navigate this new frontier.

Read Proverbs 29:20. Have you ever posted something on social media in anger, frustration, retort, or haste (including pictures), hitting "post" before your cooler head prevailed? What happened?

My name is Jen Hatmaker and I am a hothead. Information sears me quickly and dramatically … but always recedes after walking away and getting my head on straight. My knee-jerk response can almost never be trusted. I wait at least a day to respond to harsh criticism, post a controversial blog, or pile on a volatile issue online. Not because I am so wise, but because I've made an idiot out of myself one too many times, and I'm sick of saying I'm sorry.

Social media is unprecedented, because truly, once that picture goes up, it's on there forever. Once you comment, it's recorded for infinity. After you thrust your opinions onto the World Wide Web, that intellectual property is no longer yours. Relationships can be destroyed. Trust can be violated. Feelings can be wrecked. Reputations can be ruined. It's never been so easy to injure one another and ourselves.

Just wait. Pause. Shut your laptop. Take a walk. Sleep on it. Breathe deeply. Keep it as a draft. Don't publish yet. Discuss it with a safe confidant first. I cannot tell you how differently most hotbeds feel to me by the next morning. (If you could see some of the unsent drafts I have, you would put me on your prayer chains.)

But how do we deal with hate or ignorance or foolishness online, assuming we're not hasty or rash?

Read Proverbs 26:4. Now read verse 5. (Solomon juked us!) Remember our weapons: truth, discernment, Holy Spirit. On social media, how do you determine when to abide by verse 4 and when to follow verse 5?

I recently wrote a blog on white privilege in America, because being popular is very important to me (see also: my blogs on Santa, the Stop Kony Campaign, and post-adoption rules for strangers). Some blog replies were so offensive, I removed them immediately from my blog and brain. Good-bye. No room in the inn for crazies. Not gonna take the bait. Refuse to engage a pointless debate with an angry, screaming lunatic.

Others took information out of context, misquoted me, and railed against things I didn't actually say, but I responded because I sensed a desire for discussion. I saw a chance to clarify my position, ask questions, and promote civil dialogue. While some responses were unmeasured and assumptive, there were indicators for engaging them toward productive discourse.

Sometimes we need to be verse 4 responders, and other times verse 5 is in order. (And sometimes we're the fools, in which case, BE COOL, EVERYONE.) Ask yourself: *Is this healthy? Could this be productive? Is this person harming herself or others? Could this become a conversation or just an argument? If this was my son or daughter, would I hope someone would lovingly confront them on this posted content?*

Read Proverbs 26:22. Has social media increased your impulse to gossip? If so, how?

I want to tell you this hasn't affected me, but I would be lying. Let's face it; with the information and pictures some unabashedly post, we've never had a deeper gossip well to draw from. (Dear Social Media Users, please stop posting pics of your ovulation kit. Thank you.) I wish I were above this temptation and only used social media for orphan advocacy and Bible study, but I know more about people than I've ever known, even when I knew them in real life. And all that knowing is a lot to keep a lid on.

In some cases, certain online friends are gossipmongers, constantly stirring the pot and passive-aggressively taking swipes at others. This clearly applies to social sites entirely devoted to gossip, preying on celebrities and headliners, posting fascinating pictures of them walking down the street or walking up the street or walking across the street. Social media has taken "talking about people" to a whole new level.

Let's just not do it. We don't have to share everything we read. We can unfriend, unfollow, or unsubscribe from unhealthy natterers … or we can stop being one. Let's put a lid on it. We are going to make social media safer or poisonous.

Poor and Scarce

Social media takes time. Sometimes a lot of time. Time that could be spent productively elsewhere.

Read Proverbs 6:6–11. What forms of "poverty" and "scarcity" can too much social media inflict on us?

Ladies and gentlemen, we've arrived at the portion of today's show that applies most to me. I have a weird life, connected to tens of thousands of people through writing and through social media. In the most precious, endearing ways, I'm connected to readers, conference attenders, and new friends with one click. Not to mention my regular friends, of which there are tons.

Time. This all takes time. Responding, replying, forging connections, answering questions, posting important information about kale smoothies and hair products; these take a substantial chunk of my day. I recently hit emotional bankruptcy from it all, disconnected from my family and real-life friends and running on fumes. I simply could not turn it off but felt compelled to remain plugged in lest one comment got away from me. Solomon was right: I felt the poverty of real flesh-and-blood community. I experienced the scarcity of peace and privacy and still spaces and fresh air and healthy family rhythms.

Lots of experts are weighing in here. It turns out, all this input isn't just distracting; it's troubling. A recent *New York Times* article, citing dozens of sources, reported that *this is your brain on computers*:

> Scientists say juggling e-mail, phone calls and other incoming information can change how people think and behave. They say our ability to focus is being undermined by bursts of information. ...
>
> The stimulation provokes excitement—a dopamine squirt—that researchers say can be addictive. In its absence, people feel bored. The resulting distractions can have deadly consequences, as when cell phone-wielding drivers and train engineers cause wrecks. ... And for millions of people ... these urges can inflict nicks and cuts on creativity and deep thought, interrupting work and family life.[2]

Even after this multitasking ends, fractured thinking persists; because evidently *this is also your brain off computers*. Researchers at Stanford found that media multitaskers seem more sensitive to incoming information than nonmultitaskers, and that is not necessarily good:

> A portion of the brain acts as a control tower, helping a person focus and set priorities. More primitive parts of the brain, like those that process sight and sound, demand that it pay attention to new information, bombarding the control tower when ... stimulated.
>
> Researchers say there is an evolutionary rationale for the pressure this barrage puts on the brain. The lower-brain functions alert humans to danger, like a nearby lion, overriding goals like building a hut. In the modern world, the chime of incoming e-mail can override the goal of writing a business plan or playing catch with the children.[3]

Do you ever experience this input overload, constantly checking alternative sites, sources, accounts, and feeds? What does this look like for you?

Does social media activity decrease your productivity? How has this week of media fasting affected it?

During our month unplugged, I felt like I took a deep breath for the first time in ages. I discovered I can go offline, and no one will die. I can set boundaries, and the earth will continue to rotate. I am not nearly as essential to the social media universe as I thought. News flash.

Even better, time was reclaimed, repurposed toward family and friends. The input addiction loosened its grip. I got stuff done, y'all. We looked each other in the eyes. We took "walks" meaning we stopped every 20 feet to talk to neighbors. We read books, and by "we" I mean Sydney, Caleb, and me. (I begged God for readers; I am currently three for five, but the campaign is not over.) We cooked, played games, hung out with friends, got our work done, and lived life.

I don't want to be a slave to media any more than I want to be a slave to the dollar. The first time Paul mentioned permissibility to the Corinthians, he wrote: "'I will not be brought under the control of anything" (1 Cor. 6:12b). It will take conscious work to resist the control of media; its ideologies, paradigms, worldviews, and temptations, not to mention the potential substitution of genuine community with digital community. But I think if we shut down some of the noise and static, we might find more God, more neighborly love, more family, more life. May we be only under the control of Jesus who fills our minds with hope and truth and grace unending.

After fasting and studying this week, have you identified any permanent changes or reforms for media intake in your home? Do you have a specific area to focus on? What did you hear from the Spirit this week? All responses are welcome. He leads us uniquely, each one of us.

Want More?

- Make permanent screen-free zones or time blocks in your home.
- Declare one day a week completely screen-free, and use that time to serve, invite neighbors or coworkers over, or enjoy Family Night.
- Do you have an account or media outlet that owns you in an unhealthy way? Delete it.
- Go through your social media sites and purge anyone who is toxic, destructive, or unhealthy.
- Unsubscribe to the vendors, organizations, and blogs who send you automatic e-mails, tempting you to spend more time, money, or energy on superfluous things (this could include "good" things).

- Need a radical change? Cut back or cut off cable altogether.
- Put a lovely bowl near your front door for family and guests to leave their cell phones. Post a sign next to it: "Be with the ones who are here."
- Purge those stacks and drawers full of CDs, movies, video games, and DVDs. Donate them to an underresourced day care, community center, youth facility, library, children's shelter, or hospital.
- Get rid of a few TVs, gaming systems, phones, or computers in your house. Less screens = less time plugged in.
- Purge your DVR. (Please don't delete "Friday Night Lights" though.)

Wrap Up

My husband, Brandon, shares his thoughts wrapping up our media fast:

> One of Peter's early leadership lessons from Jesus was about letting go. He said the things we hold loosely are more likely to have eternal impact than the things we bind. When we hold too tightly to things, we lose perspective as well. While Jesus was talking about the kingdom in this passage, His words certainly give us insight to our created nature.
>
> We like our stuff. We need our things. Usually the things we think we need become the very things we need a break from. This was the case for me with media.
>
> Media has changed the way we interact with one another and what we spend our time doing. Our social norms have changed. The pressure is on. ...

What began as advances in the ease of communication has become something that clutters and consumes. Media "noise" is everywhere, and some perspective would probably do us all some good.

This month came with a surprisingly high level of prep work: Updates on social media warning my peeps I was taking a break, scouting the month for any critical sporting events, and getting any necessary projects or anticipated recreational media out of the way before we started. In hindsight, this was feasible because I knew it was only a month. Truth is, most of us could do anything for a month, but very few of us could do without media for much longer. Like my dad refusing to learn e-mail or own a cell phone, it's unrealistic to expect society to reorient their norms around any of us.

That said, while beginning this month of *Seven* was harder for me than the others (and I gave Jen a harder time about it), it became a refreshing break from the norm. Everyone was respectable—if not envious—of my Twitter and Facebook "fast," few cared whether or not I watched TV, and surfing the Internet had honestly already lost it's flair for me. Honestly, my biggest fear going into media month was that the world might stop turning until I was done, but I discovered others didn't need me to be as wired as I thought. Most of my media involvement is simply about me (blah). ...

All told, media month offered some pretty good perspective. Someone once said, "Think about the things you'd most hate to lose (outside of your family) and you'll identify your idols." These are not only the things we treasure too much, but what we've likely lost perspective on. ... If we're not careful, TV can become this. Facebook and Twitter can become this. Even the unreasonable pressure to respond to every e-mail immediately can become this.

The dangerous part of our social media and technologically saturated world is not its existence, but what it distracts us from. We found quality time with family, focused attention to conversation, and creativity in planning our weeknights and weekends; all refreshing additions to our month. And while the Hatmaker clan resumed a very abridged schedule of TV and Internet and gaming, we certainly gained a new perspective on them all.[4]

How did your fast from media and technology go this week? What did you learn about yourself? What did you notice about your habits? What was difficult? What was surprising? How did God speak in the empty space? Any breakthroughs? Any disappointments? What will you take away?

Week 6

WASTE

GAS

Video Notes

Group Guide

How does creation remind you of your Creator God?

How do we abuse the natural resources God has provided to us?

Have you experienced a time when natural resources were less abundant (for example: after a natural disaster, on a foreign mission trip, etc.)? Describe the circumstances.

What can you do differently to better steward creation? What tangible steps can you take?

Video session downloads available at www.lifeway.com/jenhatmaker

Getting Ready for Waste

The Bible and I are all ready to turn you into tree-hugging, dreadlock-wearing, organic-farming, compost-producing hippies (kidding … mostly), but let's nail down your personal fast from wasting first.

In the original 7 experiment, we started from utter scratch, meaning we didn't conserve anything. Ever. Not perishables, product materials, natural resources, energy, water, gas, nothing. We were wasters. We were definitely a part of the problem. I no more thought about how my consumption affected the earth or anyone else living on it than I thought about becoming a personal trainer; there was just no category for it in my mind. I completely separated God the Creator from, ahem, creation, assuming His top priority was to make His followers comfortable and prosperous, and if we needed to consume the rest of creation to make us happy, I was sure He didn't mind.

Soooo … we adopted the following seven habits for a month:

Gardening* Composting Conserving energy and water

Recycling (everything, all of it)

Driving only one car (for the love of the land)

Shopping thrift and second-hand Buying only local

*Since I had the advantage of foresight, we prepped our garden two months in advance. Our fast from waste fell helpfully in July, so the garden was magnificent. You may be studying this week in December in Michigan and all this was sprung on you, in which case we need to punt. (By the way, Wary Potential Gardeners, I never kept a plant alive in my life until 7. I'd gardened *never*. We were total morons and still managed to grow food, so please act impressed and don't disqualify yourself because you have a personal history of murdering plant life.)

If this category is old hat to you, thank you for indulging those of us late to the party. If it is uncharted territory, thank you for suspending cynicism or apathy to respect the earth God made and loves, caring for it in a way that makes sense for your kids and our kids and everyone's kids.

Have a Come to Jesus Meeting with your people, particularly if you expect them to stop throwing water bottles in the trash and share one car this week. I kindly noted for my tribe that "buying only local" eliminated Chick-Fil-A, Starbucks, Target, and other cherished vendors, which they were *thrilled* about (sarcasm). Get your gang on board according to the boundaries you've chosen and roll up your sleeves, gentle reader … we're off to become granola people.

You can tackle all or some of the waste reforms this week, or here are some other options:

Eliminate seven convenience products that contribute to landfills/deforestation/pollution like: paper towels, water bottles, sandwich baggies, paper plates, fast food and coffee (bags, napkins, plastic silverware, wrappers, Styrofoam cups), plastic grocery bags, and soda cans.

Take inventory of your fridge, pantry, cleaning supplies, and bathroom products. Assess and address the following seven areas:

1. What items come heavily packaged with multiple layers of plastic and cardboard?
2. What could you buy in bulk rather than individual packages?
3. Can you buy a concentrated product and simply add water and reuse an old spray bottle or container?
4. With what products could you reduce plastic consumption (one of the worst offenders)?
5. Where can you replace paper with cloth?
6. What products are unnecessary and could be eliminated altogether?
7. What containers could be reused?

After discussing with your spouse, family, roommates, or partners in crime, how have you decided to fast from waste this week?

What are your concerns?

Enemies No Longer

If I'm taking cues from many mainstream evangelicals, then only left-wing, loosey-goosey liberals care about the earth. Ecology is for alarmists who want to ruin our lives and obsess about acid rain, right? Plus, it's all a big scam. The earth is *fine*.

This was my position before 7.

Now I'm beginning to wonder if the unprecedented consumption of the earth's resources and the cavalier destruction of its natural assets is a spiritual issue as much as environmental. Like Wendell Berry wrote: "The ecological teaching of the Bible is simply inescapable: God made the world because He wanted it made. He thinks the world is good, and He loves it. It is His world; He has never relinquished title to it. And He has never revoked the conditions, bearing on His gift to us of the use of it, that oblige us to take excellent care of it. If God loves the world, then how might any person of faith be excused for not loving it or justified in destroying it?"[1]

I cannot explain why we've pitted God and science against each other so violently, since one was the Creator of the other and our knowledge of creation is ever unfolding; we need not be so threatened. Science couldn't possibly disprove God (what could?) but only our interpretations and theories. When science advances and reveals something we didn't know before, something we understood incorrectly, it doesn't mean God was wrong; it means we were. Believers once thought the earth was flat and sin caused blindness.

Specifically, I'm perplexed by the cynical dismissal of creation care by Christians who, according to our Bible, should be stewarding, valuing, and protecting this beautiful planet God took such great pains with. (To be fair, many Christians have long waved the green flag.) Some are surprised the Bible actually has much to say here. Perhaps in this case, we should examine Scripture as the message of Christianity rather than the behavior of Christians as its ambassadors. The color *green* has been maligned and stripped of every good meaning it ever enjoyed. We must redeem it because, in Jesus' name, it is ours.

There are so many verses about God's world, His love for it, its beauty and fruitfulness, us as stewards, creation as precious, I hardly know where to begin. When we stipulate that God actually made the earth, perhaps we can start with His feelings about the whole enterprise.

The Book of Job includes a moving section after Job's three friends accused him of sin, injustice, and other failures responsible for all his sorrow. By the end of their lectures, we find Job confused, frustrated, sarcastic, and broken, certain God had abandoned him.

To answer Job's accusation of abandonment, God stepped into the story with any number of arguments at His disposal. He could've explained Job's predicament in clear terms, which He never did (seriously, God?). He could've taken the gentle, restorative approach since clearly *Job had borne a bad run.* He could've commended Job on his upright life and endurance of such profound loss. God could've certainly offered nice reassurance about how, no, He did *not* abandon Job; He never abandons us.

Instead, this is how God answered.

Read Job 38:1–15. How did God demonstrate His presence and sovereignty?

Skim through chapters 38–41. What tone do you pick up on as God describes His creation? What stands out to you?

That's a lot of divine detail. It sounds to me like God loves this earth. He even talks sort of fierce about it. "Everything under heaven belongs to Me" (41:11). Beautiful descriptors: the proud waves, the dawn He showed its place, drops of dew, the constellations in their seasons, the Bear with its cubs, the horse's flowing mane, the soaring eagle, wild animals playing nearby. (Wow. God should be a writer.)

Many dismiss this topic, claiming the earth is here for our temporary use and consumption; restraint need not apply, because God wrote us a blank ecological check to cash in at will. Certainly God designed the earth to sustain life, including human life. There is no question this planet feeds, shelters, and nourishes us with aplomb.

But read Job 38:24-27,33. What point do you think God is making?

How have you historically viewed this topic?

Stealing from Peter to Pay Paul

If it sounds for one moment like I am judging, let me assure you I'm not. I'm so not. My first pass at any of this was during 7. I have 35 other years I can't account for. My frustration is with myself and the political nattering that set Christians up as adversaries to environmentalists, which I totally bought.

I can hear the arguments now:
- Worship the Creator, not the created.
- It's all New Age and steeped in mysticism.
- Global warming will not annihilate the earth. God will. So I'm not messing with it.
- This earth is not eternal. Why "Save the Planet" when God eventually will destroy it?
- We're here to love people, not the earth.
- This is a liberal agenda. (To do what? Take care of what we've abdicated? And it's bad because "they" care about it? Since when are Christians an "us" politically? This issue does not belong to any political party but to the people of God.)
- Environmentalists don't shave their legs. That's weird.

OK, I added that last one, but still. I wonder if we enjoy such a cavalier attitude about creation care because we're so removed from the effects of its squandering? We are Americans. We are above the nuisance of depleted resources. We'll just buy more. Surely there is always more.

Few of us actually rely on the land we can see and touch. We don't feel the repercussions of deforestation. We don't swim in the ocean's trash swirl. We get our water from nine faucets in our homes. Our pets aren't going extinct. Crop failures don't affect us. Our grocery stores are infinite. Oil consumption? Who cares? There is always gas at our pumps. Well, maybe …

> There is not always more … Except for our energy income from the sun, the world is finite. Numbers of individual organisms … may seem limitless, but they are not. Species may appear to be beyond counting, … but they are finite in number. Our life support systems … may seem beyond abuse, but there are limits to what they can bear. Like it or not, we are finite creatures living in a finite world.[2]

In fact, according to the *Living Planet Report 2008*, more than three-quarters of the world's people are living in nations that are ecological debtors, where national consumption has outstripped their country's biological capacity. Presently, human demands on the world's natural capital measure 30 percent more than earth can sustain. Global consumption of natural resources far exceeds the earth's regenerative capacity. We are borrowing from our natural capital at an entirely unsustainable rate. Most of us are propping up our current lifestyles, and our economic growth, by drawing—and increasingly overdrawing—*on the ecological capital of other parts of the world.*[3]

Guess who has the largest global footprint? Together with China, America accounts for 40 percent of the earth's depletion. "If our demands on the planet continue to increase at the same rate, by the mid-2030s we would need the equivalent of two planets to maintain our lifestyles," according to World Wildlife Fund International Director-General James Leape.[4]

America's global footprint is made up of millions of people like me, making choices that affect the planet, getting defensive when the rest of earth's citizens quietly say, "Please. Please stop. You are deficit spending our shared resources and there is no bailout if the earth's systems collapse."

The 7 Experiment is addressing irresponsible consumption. It's sometimes easier to acknowledge food or clothes or possessions than waste. Why do you think this category of consumption is harder to confront?

The Theology of Ecology

Perhaps we've divorced the two, but God made repetitive connections biblically between the state of society and the state of the earth. In Scripture, nature operates as a powerful medium of God's presence or absence. Hills leap for joy and rivers clap their hands in God's presence. Or, conversely, nature grows hostile and barren as an indicator of divine wrath. I mean, in response to the very first sin on earth, God cursed the ground, predicting much toil through its thorns and thistles.

Sin literally hurt the earth. Hold that thought …

The modern worldview that set human reason outside and above nature, treating it as an object reduced to human control, is the heart of modern exploitation, but it does not properly correspond to the biblical vision of the environment. Any recovery of an appropriate interpretation begins by critiquing where we've gone wrong in our relationship to God's good gift of the earth. Perhaps the vision of Israel's prophets provides the germ of that critical and prophetic vision. There are so many passages with similar language, but let's just pick one.

Read God's judgment on society in Isaiah 24:1–13. What are some of the abuses God catalogues to cause such ecological despair?

In this view, nature is part of the covenant between God and mankind; the entire earth falls under God's punishment. We are integrated in every spiritual way. Creation is a mirror reflecting human social and spiritual ills. The two are profoundly linked together as parts of one covenant, so that, more and more, the disasters of nature become less a purely natural fact and increasingly a social fact.

(Skim through the Prophets and notice God's constant ecological language through the peaks and valleys of redemption and rebellion.)

There is no way to interpret Isaiah other than the profile of an unjust society. When God said in 24:5-6, "The earth is defiled by its people; they have disobeyed the laws, violated the statutes and broken the everlasting covenant. Therefore a curse consumes the earth; its people must bear their guilt" (NIV), He had already made an ironclad case against them in the Book of Isaiah.

- Your hands are full of blood (see 1:15).
- You do not defend the fatherless or widow (see 1:23).
- Your land is full of silver and gold. There is no end to your treasures (see 2:7).
- You are arrogant and proud (see 2:17).
- The plunder from the poor is in your houses (see 3:14).
- You're grinding the faces of the poor (see 3:15).
- You have no respect for the work of My hands (see 5:12).
- You are denying justice to the innocent (see 5:23).
- You deprive the poor of their rights, withhold justice from the oppressed, make widows your prey, and rob the fatherless (see 10:2).

If creation is a spiritual mirror, what does the earth currently communicate about the level of injustice God's people are allowing and perpetuating?

The connection is practically assumed: If we are at odds with God, then we are likely at odds with the poor, which makes us at odds with nature. Why does rebellion against God automatically indicate neglect of the poor? (I spy a theme.)

So if this flow chart starts for better or worse with our respect for God—not the poor, not creation—what does our subsequent disrespect of people and nature possibly indicate?

The response of nature to human use and abuse is not just spiritually symbolic. When we exploit the labor of the worker and plunder natural resources and deny the social costs of production and poison our air and water and exhaust the earth's forests, the poor are profoundly affected. The depleted earth isn't just an indicator of injustice; it is an injustice itself. The impact of environmental degradation falls most heavily on the people who are least able to mitigate these impacts—poor and vulnerable populations. It also disproportionately affects fragile plants, animals, and ecosystems.

Read Isaiah 24:7-11 again. What picture did God paint of His people before this judgment?

What connections do you see between this description and our current emotional temperature in regard to the earth and its poor?

Cobra Pits and Snake Dens: Safe for Children!

I'm so happy to tell you this tale of desolation isn't the end of the vision. When we mend our relationship with God, rightly interpreting and obeying His mission, the ensuing recovery of just relations between people restores peace to society and, in that, heals nature's enmity. Just, peaceful societies in which God is worshiped and people are not exploited create peaceful, harmonious and beautiful natural environments.[5]

Read Isaiah 11:1-9. Jesus ushered in a new kingdom. What do you see here regarding the poor as well as creation under Jesus' leadership?

Is this the Peaceable Kingdom? Justice delivered for the poor and oppressed; the earth purged of inequity; nature experiences the loss of hostility between animal and animal, between animal and man; the wolf cohabitates with the lamb, the leopard lies down with the goat, the baby animals frolic together, little children shall lead them, play with them, sleep near them.[6]

"None will harm or destroy another on My entire holy mountain." Isaiah 11:9

Good reader, I have harmed others by refusing responsibility here, prioritizing convenience over good citizenship. My luxuries come at the expense of some of God's best handiwork: forests, petroleum, clean air, healthy ecosystems. We also ravage the lands of vulnerable countries, stripping their resources for consumption. The wealthy world has a sordid history of colonization, ruling by force over indigenous people and profiting from their natural resources and local labor. Yes Africa, we'll take your diamonds, gold, and oil, but you can keep your crushing poverty and disease.

Can we unlearn our destructive habits and re-imagine a way to live lighter on this earth? What if we changed our label from "consumers" to "stewards"? Would it change the way we shop? The way we think? What does it mean to be a godly consumer? What if God's creation is more than just a commodity? If we acknowledged the sacredness of creation, I suspect it would alter the way we treated it:

> There are a limited number of resources in this world, and when we take more than we need, simply put, we are stealing from others. … To my dismay, I realized that even in my own, sort-of-green world, I was stealing from people, present and future. Turns out I constantly steal from my kids (and yours). I'm snatching up goodies like clean air and water while millions of families clamor for a drink and struggle with disease. I'm throwing away excess paper and packaging while rain forests disappear. I'm a kleptomaniac. But I am determined to address my failings.[7]

I am determined. Shouldn't we all be?

Read Colossians 1:15–20. List everything God is restoring, redeeming, and reconciling throughout the story of creation, from beginning to end.

Creation care is a prophetic opportunity for the church. Theologically, our response here has great effect. According to Scripture, it is fully integrated with appropriate worship, justice for the poor, and a healed land. We do God's story a great disservice to relegate creation care to the margins, imagining it has nothing to do with discipleship or redemption or worship or holiness. We look to a new future, brought about by social repentance and conversion to divine commandments, so that the covenant of creation can be rectified and God's Shalom brought to nature and society. Just as mankind and nature grows hostile through injustice, so it will be restored to harmony through righteousness.[8]

May we join God in this worthy mission.

How has this week's study landed? What is your response to creation care?

What tensions do you carry?

Has Scripture moved you in a new way, or have you seen something fresh? What is the next right thing to do? You can safely and honestly pray about this. God is for us, ever drawing us closer and more deeply into His mission.

Want More?

- Figure out ways to drive less (emissions are one of the top offenders, not to mention gas consumption): set up a carpool, broker some "work from home" time, choose driving days and consolidate all errands, trade driving days with your spouse and use the same car.
- Feel like getting serious? Get rid of an extra car.
- Drive a gas guzzler? Consider trading it. (We got a Suburban that uses flex fuel.)
- If it is possible, commit to using urban transit.
- Extend this waste fast to a month if it needs more time to marinate.
- Commit to buying only locally or thrift for six months.
- Find out if there are any community gardens in your city and join one or volunteer. Take your kids.
- Join a Community Supported Agriculture (CSA).
- Make permanent reforms on how you buy food: less packaging, less single-use products, less Big Ag products, more local in-season produce, more local meat and dairy, more bulk items, more reusable containers.
- Prepare and plan for a garden if the timing was off this week. Gentle reader, if I can do it, a monkey can do it. Weather and timing off? No yard? Plant a small indoor herb garden. It's still amazing to watch stuff grow and eat it.

Tackle paper consumption. The average American household receives more than 500 pieces of advertising mail each year, and of the 5.56 million tons shipped, only 1.23 million tons are recycled.[9] That's a lot of waste.

1. Get off most national marketing lists by registering with the Direct Marketing Association's Mail Preference Service (*www.DMAchoice.org*). This doesn't take five minutes.
2. Unsubscribe from unsolicited catalogues.
3. Call 1-888-5-OPT-OUT to reach the major national credit bureaus, Equifax, Experian, and Trans Union to stop mailings of credit card offers.
4. Think outside the paper book:
   - Get a library card and borrow books rather than buy.
   - E-readers are also a savvy new way to reduce paper usage and *still read*.
   - Newspaper reader? Cancel your subscription and read the paper online.

Wrap Up

I'm sick with despair at all I left out this week.

I wish I had more space to include my failings, struggles, and lessons here. I didn't even get to tell you about gardening.

And composting.

And driving one car except that one day when we didn't because of *pee-wee football practice*.

Building a biblical case for creation care took the cake in this study, but don't imagine I didn't slosh and slug my own way through this.

As you prepare to mine your conclusions, please enjoy my wrap up from the original 7 experiment:

> Oh my stars, has this month ever lodged deeply!
>
> I keep thinking about our obsession with health. Our kids have been immunized, checked, prodded, measured, tested, and examined since the day they were born. Cuts get antibacterial crème and Band-Aids. Twisted ankles get ice. Strep throats get antibiotics. We fuel our bodies with good food, drinking enough water and milk to keep the wheels on. Brandon and I make sure our parents get annual checkups, and we visit the dentist twice a year. I'm watching for tricky moles and checking for lumps. I inspect my kids' lymph nodes and keep us all sunscreened. We have a cabinet of pills if something veers off course, and I can pick up a prescription one hour after a diagnosis.
>
> Why?
>
> Because God gave us spectacular bodies and we value them.
>
> But as certainly as God created man in His image, He first created the earth. With the same care He designed 60,000 miles of blood vessels in the human body, He also crafted hydrangeas and freshwater rapids and hummingbirds. He balanced healthy ecosystems with precision and established climates and beauty. He integrated

colors and smells and sounds that would astound humanity. The details He included while designing the earth are so extraordinary, it is no wonder He spent five of the six days of creation on it.

So why don't we care for the earth anywhere near to the degree we do our bodies? Why don't we fuss and examine and steward creation with the same tenacity? Why aren't we refusing complicity in the ravaging of our planet? Why aren't we determined to stop pillaging the earth's resources like savages? Why do we mock environmentalists and undermine their passion for conservation? Do we think ourselves so superior to the rest of creation that we are willing to deplete the earth to supply our luxuries? If so, we may very well be the last generation who gets that prerogative. ...

I've been gobbling up the goodies, making a huge mess and assuming someone else would clean it up and foot the bill. But let me tell you, this month put the brakes on that. I cannot believe how God has captured me for creation care. All of it: recycling, using less, gardening, composting, conserving, buying local, repurposing instead of replacing; I'm in. From the nearly empty garbage bin to the lower electric bill, the immediate effects of a greener lifestyle are obvious.

My land, do we have far to go! My hypocrisies are too numerous to count, but this month birthed something unmistakable: I'm done separating ecology from theology, pretending they don't originate from the same source. "The earth is the LORD's, and everything in it, the world, and all who live in it; for he founded it on the seas and established it on the waters" (Ps. 24:1-2, NIV).

A friend said, "I don't know why you're trying. It won't matter. No one else cares." To that, I'll close with this bit of wisdom:

"If God is really at the center of things and God's good future is the most certain reality, then the truly realistic course of action is to buck the dominant consequentialist ethic of our age—which says that we should act only if our action will most likely bring about good consequences—and simply, because we are people who embody the virtue of hope, do the right thing. If we believe it is part of our task as earthkeepers to recycle, then we ought to recycle, whether or not it will change the world. Do the right thing.

If we think it part and parcel of our ecological obedience to drive less and walk more, then that is what we ought to do. Do the right thing. … We should fulfill our calling to be caretakers of the earth regardless of whether global warming is real or there are holes in the ozone layer or three nonhuman species become extinct each day. Our vocation is not contingent on results or the state of the planet. Our calling simply depends on our identity as God's response-able human image-bearers."[10]

Let's do the right thing.[11]

How did your fast from waste go this week? What did you learn about yourself? What did you notice about your habits? What was difficult? What was surprising? How did God speak in the empty space? Any breakthroughs? Any disappointments? What will you take away?

Week 7

SPENDING

Video Notes

Group Guide

If someone looked over your checkbook, what would they say your spending priorities are? Does this assessment accurately reflect your heart?

How do your spending habits need to change? If you curbed spending, how might you reallocate the savings?

Has God drawn you to a need or people group or cause? What could you do differently with your spending to support this effort?

Video session downloads available at www.lifeway.com/jenhatmaker

Getting Ready for Spending

I like this week, because unlike "possessions" which involved money already doled out (exhausting me with regret), spending is present and future; our history need not inform what is to come. Spending offers us a blank slate, and I don't know about you, but 7 made me ravenous for a fresh start. But before we get into it, it's time to decide on your personal fast.

Once upon a time, preparing for this month of 7, I averaged the previous year's bank statements and totaled how many places we spent money not including repeat expenditures: 66 vendors a month. Then I totally spazzed out. The end. Anyone who spends money in 66 places a month is the most heinous kind of consumer. Had you asked me to estimate, I would've guessed less than half of what we actually frittered away. So we chose the following seven vendors, and only these seven, for a month:

The Sunset Valley Farmer's Market   HEB gas station (flex fuel!)

Online bill pay   Kids' school   Limited travel fund   Emergency medical   Target*

*Target was the all-purpose back on my roster, because it was August and there was a (slight) chance the weather would turn, and my kids' jeans neither buttoned nor covered their shins. And for other glitches (like toilet paper and detergent). However, we attempted to meet our needs any other way before traipsing off to Target (as I could sustain our entire life there without missing a step). I'm happy to tell you I only went once and spent less than $50, which is the single time in history that has ever happened.

One other note: we enacted the "giving clause," which exempted charitable spending from consumerism, benefitting someone's actual needs rather than my endless wants. So we continued to sponsor kids in India and Zimbabwe, tithe, and give to service projects without counting them in our seven line items.

I only spent on travel twice (I had two events in other states), and we never used the emergency medical option. "School" was a totally unfun choice (we can't go 14 seconds without sending field trip fees, lunch money, class T-shirt dues, or recorder payments), but our plumb line was: If we might need to spend somewhere, we have to count it.

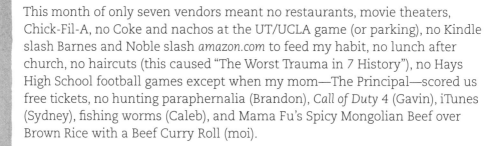

This month of only seven vendors meant no restaurants, movie theaters, Chick-Fil-A, no Coke and nachos at the UT/UCLA game (or parking), no Kindle slash Barnes and Noble slash *amazon.com* to feed my habit, no lunch after church, no haircuts (this caused "The Worst Trauma in 7 History"), no Hays High School football games except when my mom—The Principal—scored us free tickets, no hunting paraphernalia (Brandon), *Call of Duty 4* (Gavin), iTunes (Sydney), fishing worms (Caleb), and Mama Fu's Spicy Mongolian Beef over Brown Rice with a Beef Curry Roll (moi).

As I was preparing for this month, my friends made the hilarious suggestion that I double up on options (use the gas station at the grocery store, buy lunch at Target, etc.), so I could squeeze more mileage out of my seven retailers and slip at least one restaurant in the rotation. I ignored them because I wanted this month to pinch, but if you'd like to follow their wily ways, you can work in as many multipurpose vendors as you'd like.

We obviously looped our kids into this one, as they are a huge spending line item, but apply this to your family in whatever manner makes sense. Again, there are plenty of means to the same end, and our habits are all different.

Choose seven places to spend this week, or try one of these alternatives:

- Eliminate seven well-trafficked vendors that usually get your expendable dough.
- Choose seven alternatives of nonconsumption (pack lunch, eat dinner at home every night, walk/carpool rather than drive, take a walk with your friend rather than meet for lunch or coffee, etc.)

- Eliminate seven categories of spending (restaurants, clothes, home accessories, beauty/personal appearance, entertainment, etc.)
- Choose seven organizations, nonprofits, or missions to spend on this week rather than your usual fare.

After discussing with your spouse, family, roommates, or partners in crime, how have you decided to fast from spending this week?

What are your concerns?

Hey, Big Spender

When Brandon and I married in college, our joint income was $11,270. We were so poor, people on welfare gave *us* cheese and peanut butter. This trend continued through the early days of youth ministry and into the lean days of one-income, babies, and toddlers. I remember Brandon handing me a 20-dollar bill to feed us for a week. The refrigerator and pantry were empty; I had a preschooler at the table, a toddler on my leg, and a baby on my hip. I sat in the middle of our kitchen and bawled my eyes out.

Back then, we didn't just watch each penny; we scrutinized, counted, shuffled, and squeezed every last one. Sonic was an outrageous extravagance. Staying true to our generation, we dug a deep, dark debt hole to purchase the lifestyle we couldn't afford but for some reason felt entitled to. Unwilling to live within our means, we lived paycheck to paycheck, floating checks and nodding politely as the wealthy people at church talked about their vacations and new cars, wondering who we had to know to acquire these luxuries (Chase and Capital One were happy to oblige).

A few years go by—yada yada yada—and I'm spending in 66 places a month. Heaven help. Combing through a year of bank statements, we were not big-ticket item buyers; we nickeled-and-dimed ourselves to death. We spent almost everything we made, and honestly, I could barely account for half of it.

This is why spending flew under my radar; it was subtle, incremental, seemingly inconsequential. Just this little thing here, and that small thing there; I don't feel like cooking, let's just get this. Individually, nothing too egregious, but together, our spending amounted to a startling number.

Spending is the precursor to possessions, and Jesus said possessions will steer our hearts, so let's lay the ax at the root of the tree.

Want to work with real numbers? Tally up the last six months of bank statements and average the number of vendors per month. (This is how I discovered our absurd financial relationship with restaurants.)

What did you notice? Any surprises, good or bad?

Big deal, right? Do I really need to care about this high-end lipstick? Does it actually hurt someone if I buy these jeans or help someone if I don't? Let's say I cut spending down and work toward less consumption. So what? Is there even a chance my choices would matter?

I think they might.

Let's consider some of our spending tendencies:
- Annual US spending on cosmetics: $8 billion
- Annual US and European spending on pet food: $17 billion
- Annual US and European spending on perfume: $12 billion

Now let's look at some other global totals:
- Clean water for all global citizens: $9 billion
- Basic education for all global children: $6 billion
- Basic health and nutrition for all: $13 billion[1]

Some may argue that it is more expensive to live in the Western civilization, but consider this report from The United Nations:

> Today's consumption is undermining the environmental resource base. It is exacerbating inequalities. And the dynamics of the consumption-poverty-inequality-environment nexus are accelerating. If the trends continue without change … today's problems of consumption and human development will worsen.

> The real … issue is not consumption itself but its patterns and effects. Inequalities in consumption are stark. Globally, the 20% of the world's people in the highest-income countries account for 86% of total private consumption expenditures—the poorest 20% a minuscule 1.3%.[2]

That's us: That 20 percent at the top buying 86 percent of the stuff. So no, maybe one person pulling out wouldn't matter. But if hundreds and thousands then millions of us challenged the paradigm, saying no for every two times we say yes, acknowledging the power of our consumer dollar—to either battle inequality or reinforce it—then our generation could turn the ship around.

We have a list of objections to choose from:
- "It's no big deal."
- "I can afford this."
- "I've worked hard for my money, so I can spend it how I want."
- "I want this, back off."
- "I deserve this."
- "Other people spend way more." (My personal favorite.)
- "I still have money in the bank."

Do you identify with any of these sentiments? How so?

Curbing spending could go one of two ways: either we spend less to save more, or we spend less to give more. Do you lean more one way than the other? Talk about that.

Saving, Spending, and Storing: Tell Us What to Do, Jesus

Don't imagine I'm advocating for no savings. The Bible has several instructive nuggets on maintaining a cushion, saving for seasons of drought and hardship. Wisdom plans ahead (that is, if she has the luxury of expendable income; this is a First World extravagance).

But the numbers are so tipped in our favor, I wonder if God doesn't expect more from the top 20 percent (and most of us are in the top 5 percent) than simply buying 86 percent of the stuff and harboring savings accounts with the rest. I wonder if there is a graded option somewhere below our means.

As with any healthy conversation, we must look to the whole of Scripture rather than proof texting ones we like. I took an intricate view of the Bible for so long, I missed the high view, the one where God's big story comes into focus and the parts become the whole. The one where God's heart for the oppressed is in *every single book*. So when it comes to managing money, we must take a holistic approach and ask, "What is God mostly saying in Scripture?"

Luke tells us a man wanted Jesus to tell his brother to split their inheritance. Jesus wasn't dealing with a crooked lawsuit or a spat between enemies. These were brothers with a rightful claim.

Read Luke 12:13–21. Why do you think Jesus answered like He did rather than offer a practical solution?

What connection do you see between the "rightful entitlement" of these brothers and our attitude toward our wealth and advantages?

Again, Jesus took a swipe at stored possessions, which He understood to be the inevitable end of this argument. He interpreted this high level of angst correctly: it was for more stuff; this inheritance wasn't going to land in the hands of the poor. Nothing can turn humans into thrashing, clawing, desperate enemies quicker than money. With precision, Jesus identified why they were fighting (greed) and what the end result would be (hoarded wealth) without asking a single question. Money makes us super predictable.

Read verses 16–21 again. What stands out to you? What false assumptions did the man embrace?

Is this like selling perfectly lovely houses for bigger ones because our stuff outpaced our square footage? Has it become standard protocol to go bigger than live smaller? I believe we are liquid consumers, able to fill any container we pour ourselves into, no matter how spacious it feels at first.

I find Jesus' take on savings so practical. Evidently, there is a limit to what we sock away, ensuring our ease and merriment later. This flies squarely in the face of the American Dream, but Jesus apparently doesn't give one whit. I wish He would've given us a clearer formula or income-to-savings ratio, but He did give clues to check our temperature:

Relational distress, specifically among family

Greed   Abundance   Excessive wealth   Upsizing

Hoarding   Selfishness   Spiritual poverty

Striving toward ease and merriment ("Take life easy ...")

How do you need to respond to Jesus' difficult teaching?

Tithing on Mint and Rue (whatever that is)

Let's kick back over to that 86 percent of private consumption we're gobbling up. With spending responsible for this degree of inequity, we are growing deaf to Jesus who described a simple life marked by generosity and under-consumption, and over time, a new compartment has developed for our spending habits, safely distanced from the other drawers like "discipleship" and "stewardship" (which has been helpfully reduced to *tithing*).

"But I tithe" was my get-out-of-jail-free card for years. I tithed and the church proceeded to use that money for great good, right? *Right?* Oh, these fancy marble floors? The expensive landscaping? The exorbitant salaries and equipment and conferences? Well, the church has to be awesome, or who will come, for the love of Elijah?

Sidebar note: How have we let the church deteriorate like this? How is this OK? How can we endorse these expenditures? When did this become standard protocol for the Bride of Christ? We've engineered an elaborate two-step to justify this egregious spending *on ourselves*. We are far from Jesus' original vision; the whole enterprise would be unrecognizable to our early church fathers. The earth is groaning, and we're putting coffee bars in our $35 million sanctuaries. Just because we can have it doesn't mean we should. I marvel at how out of place simple, humble Jesus would be in today's American churches.

But since you don't control your church's purse strings (although you *do* get to choose a church stewarding tithe money for the greatest good, but there I go again), let's head back to that first defense: I tithe. This basic obedience exempts the rest of our spending, assuaging our consciences and checking the stewardship box. With that drawer comfortably shut, the others can be opened at our leisure.

Read Luke 11:37–45. What point is Jesus making in the last sentence of verse 42?

Jesus was the worst dinner guest ever. *Awkward.* Jesus' response is interesting because the issue at hand was hand washing, as He caught the Pharisee casting a reproving glance at His social omission. No one was talking about money. In fact, no one was talking at all. Then bam, after one sideways look from His host, Jesus launched into this searing lecture, and the very first remedy He offered was this:

"Give from what is within to the poor, and then everything is clean for you." Luke 11:41

Followed by an indictment on their meticulous tithing but neglect of justice. (Surely the other guests were like, "Who invited *this* guy?") I'm starting to wonder if Jesus actually meant that. Was He serious about sanctification through extreme generosity? Is He really advocating giving our goods to those without? I don't know if He knows this, but this would mean completely retooling the way we live and spend.

News flash, Jesus: Almost zero people I know live like this. I feel safer with the prosperity groupthink than with Jesus' ridiculous plan. The justification of the Christian community is happy to oblige me. (A recent statement following an exposé of a massive luxury purchase with church funds: "We operate in a manner that is worthy of the calling of Christ and have no apologies." Oh, Jesus endorses this extravagance? Carry on then.)

What if we're buying a bag of tricks? What if wealth and indulgence is creating a polished people rotting from the inside out, without even knowing it? Is there a reason Jesus called the rich: blind, deaf, unseeing, unhearing, and foolish? And dear readers, shall we stop imagining these sad, sorry, rich people belong to a different demographic? A brave believer admits, "He's talking about me." Look at our houses, cars, closets, our luxuries; if we are not rich, then no one is. If we aren't swept up in entitlement, indulgence, and extravagance, then Jesus is a fool and let's get back to living. If tithing the minimum and consuming the rest is OK, then we can dismiss Jesus' ideas and act obsessed about other stuff He said.

But what if?

What if we are actually called to a radical life? What if Jesus knew our Christian culture would design a lovely life template complete with all the privileges and exemptions we want, but even with that widespread approval, He still expected radical simplicity, radical generosity, radical obedience from those with ears to hear, eyes to see?

How could Jesus suggest that giving to the poor would make "everything clean"? Everything?

These Pharisees were a spiritual mess. What does this passage communicate about the relationship between extreme generosity and everything else Jesus then called out (injustice, pride, spiritual abuse, unrepentant hearts)?

Evidently just as money has the power to ruin, generosity has the power to heal. This is big.

Who Says "No"?

So, what if we addressed spending, since every new day is a blank check, and according to Jesus, potential for sanctification? Yes, we may need to address the corner we've painted ourselves into, as mortgages, credit card payments, and bills are fairly inflexible. There is one category for the things we *owe*, and it may or may not be in need of reform. Your house, your cars, your bills, your debt; we have to lie in the beds we've made or consider downsizing to a twin.

But what about the second category involving expendable income, especially if the first category is trimmed? (By the way, before 7 I would've told you we had little disposable revenue, but then I found out we spent in 66 places a month and Jesus was like, "Whatever!") I recognize two easy shifts we could make, starting today.

One, nonconsumption. This is the simplest and hardest. It takes true courage to rage against this machine. Could we be countercultural enough to say, "We're not buying that. We don't need that. We'll make do with what we have. We'll use the stuff we already own." If this causes anxiety, I'm with you, trust me. Because who else does that? Who curbs their appetites anymore? Who uses old stuff when they can buy new stuff? Who says no when they can afford to say yes?

We could. We could wisely discern needs from wants, and frankly, at least half of those line items are misfiled. We can simply stop spending so much, use what we have, borrow what we need, repurpose possessions instead of replacing them, and—the kicker—live with less. Like Barber noted, "The challenge is to demonstrate that as consumers we can know what we want and want only what we need; and that, with the rest of our lives we intend to live … in a plethora of life worlds in which consumption need play no role."[3]

What are your top categories of spending?

What might "nonconsumption" look like in those categories? Any habits need to be altered? How could you set yourself up for success here? (My girlfriend used to shop on her lunch hour, then she was like, "Um, maybe instead I'll just, well, eat lunch.")

Two, redirect money saved. Humor me: What if we lived on 75 percent of our income and gave the rest away strategically? Or what if we downsized to 50 percent, bringing fresh meaning to Jesus' command to "love our neighbor as ourselves"? Pulling out of a lopsided market is one thing; sharing our wealth with the world's vulnerable is a whole 'nother level.

Your giving can affect extraordinary change. Pick a need, country, people group, an organization focused on empowerment and sustainable independence. You could be an answer to countless prayers. The poor don't lack ambition, imagination, or intelligence; most simply lack resources. We have what they require and more than we need. We could share.

Are you drawn to a need or people group? What might radical generosity look like here?

While it is easy to become paralyzed by the world's suffering and inequalities created by corruption and greed, we actually hold immense power for change, simply by virtue of our wealth and economic independence. Because we decide where our dollars go. Never has so much wealth been so concentrated; our prosperity is unprecedented. If enough of us decided to share, we would unleash a torrent of justice to sweep away disparity, poverty, and hopelessness.

And let's not miss the personal healing extreme generosity catalyzes: "Give from what is within to the poor, and then everything is clean for you."

This reminds me of Isaiah 58:7-10.

"Is it not to share your bread with the hungry, to bring the poor and homeless into your house, to clothe the naked when you see him, and not to ignore your own flesh and blood? Then your light will appear like the dawn, and your recovery will come quickly. ... If you offer yourself to the hungry, and satisfy the afflicted one, then your light will shine in the darkness, and your night will be like noonday."

Wouldn't it be just like Jesus to heal the giver and the receiver through the same act of generosity? Doesn't it sound just like Him to finally mend our insides once we love on the outside? That to save our lives we must lose them, and the saving part doesn't happen until the losing part? Maybe the secret has been in front of our eyes all this time, but it was disguised as generosity, which seems an unlikely way to battle our own demons.

Perhaps we don't need another sermon or a deeper Bible study or a different mentor or a better church to heal what is broken inside us. It seems an endless focus on ourselves hasn't transformed us in the slightest anyway. Maybe in the crazy giving, the reckless sharing, the dangerous releasing, Jesus finally burrows into our hearts, piecing back the shards and lifting the shroud.

Maybe everything He ever said was true.

These Scriptures, this conversation, these ideas ... it's a lot. Almost every good turn begins with tension, so if you have it, God is moving. He loves you. He loves us. He has big plans for His church. How are you responding? What is God showing you? Where are you struggling?

Want more?

- Commit to no spending on clothes, toys, home décor, or any other category that has its claws in you for six months.
- Take the time to weed through your bank statements. Figure out how much you're spending and where. You may be surprised. Make changes from there.
- Engage a coffee or soda exchange: Commit to not buying your favorite drink for a month and divert the savings. (Compassion sponsorships are $38 a month. I spend that much money in one trip to Chick-Fil-A. *I have a lot of kids, y'all.*)

- Try Jesus economics ("Love your neighbor as yourself") for a period of time: Do not spend more money on yourself than you spend on the poor. Living on 50 percent of your income? That's radical.
- Commit to buying from retailers making a difference, corporations with a conscious who employ underresourced workers or cycle profits into vulnerable communities. Your dollar can be powerful.

Do "places I already owe" have an inordinate amount of power over your financial freedom to be generous? Have some hard conversations:

1. Could we do with a cheaper house?
2. Could we do with fewer (or cheaper) cars?
3. Are there services we could cut back or cut down on?
4. What must we do to get out of debt? (Off you go to Dave Ramsey. He'll get you out of debt then I'll show you how to spend all your extra money on poor people.)

Wrap Up

This month was the hardest for me. Checking spending—big, casual, small—was inordinately hard, indicative of what I cherish. The difficulty level was proportional to my entitlement. Here is my original conclusion from 7:

> This. Month. Was. *Hard*. But good. It's one of those. A good hard.
>
> Vast consumption is so ordinary, that its absence was shocking. I didn't realize how casually I "grab lunch," or "run through the book store," or "pick up that little scarf." I admit: I have a compulsion to buy something somewhere. My craving is nonspecific; it just involves being in a store or restaurant and handing my debit card over and getting something back.
>
> Specifically, I have never cooked so much. With zero restaurants on the list, I've spent 40 thousand hours in my kitchen this month, and I'm a little sick of it. That's right, the girl who loves fresh ingredients and cookbooks and sauté pans wants Chick-Fil-A sauce on a fried sandwich. I want to *not* figure out what to do with collard greens. I want to call Pizza Hut. ...
>
> I'm missing the convenience of consumption, but I've missed the camaraderie more. I've created conjoined twins out of *buying* and *connecting*. Time with another human meant eating at a restaurant or buying a four-dollar latte. ...
>
> For the first week, I holed up in my house, turning down invitations like a neurotic recluse. It didn't dawn on me to suggest an alternative connecting point. (I am slow.) Finally, I recognized *time together* was the real prize. ... Enter the rest of the month:

- Breakfast at Jenny's with four of my girlfriends.
- Lunch with my friend Stevie Jo. I pulled a sandwich right out of my purse.
- Amy, Lynde, and Alissa over for brunch. ...
- Reciprocal brunch at Amy's with Lynde and Alissa. I invited us over.
- National Night Out with my neighbors.
- Potluck dinner with my oh-so-beloved Restore Group.
- Family four square tournaments. ("Someone" is a cheater, and his name rhymes with *Paleb*.) ...

So yes, eating is still a starting player, but being in each other's homes, cooking and sharing food together is delightful. Eating a meal in a restaurant is one thing, but friends padding around barefoot in your kitchen and chopping carrots for your soup and sipping their coffee on your deck is another creature altogether. This exits the expediency of consumerism and enters the realm of hospitality.

There is something so nourishing about sharing your living space with people, where they see your junk mail pile and peewee football schedule on the fridge and pile of shoes by the front door. Opening your home says, "You are welcomed into my real life." This square footage is where we laugh and hold family meetings and make homemade corn dogs and work through meltdowns. Here is the railing our kids pulled out of the wall. This is the toilet paper we prefer. These are the pictures we frame, the books we're reading, the projects we're undertaking—the raw material of our family. It's unsanitized and truthful. We invite you into this intimate place, saturated with our family character.

Maybe this is why hospitality was big to the early church. Living life together in the sacred spaces of our homes is so unifying. When our Christian forerunners were persecuted and misunderstood, when belief in Jesus was dangerous and isolating, they had each other. They had dinner around the table. They had Sabbath together. They had soft places to fall when they traveled. Safe in the home of a fellow Christ-follower, they could breathe, pray, rest. What a gift.

So here at the end of the month, I have some sweet memories, mostly in my own and my friends' spaces. There were hilarious stories confessed around my table, which I shall go to the grave with under threat of beheading. I let my girlfriends inspect all my closets one morning, which is like going to work naked. People rummaged in my pantry and used my chopping board. I examined Amy's garden and lounged on her couch over five cups of coffee, enjoying our XM Radio Coffeehouse Channel obsession. I've dropped seven pounds, thanks to the absence of restaurant food and walks with my girlfriends. My little tribe enjoyed double the evenings around the dinner table, laughing through *High/Low* (Caleb: "My low is that my feet really stink right now"). We put a chunk of money into adoption savings and gave a few hundred away, because guess what? When you don't spend money, you have more at the end of the month. This financial wizardry is brought to you free of charge.

I've discovered reduced consumption doesn't equal reduced community or reduced contentment. There is something liberating about unplugging the machine to discover the heartbeat of life still thumping. Maybe we don't need all those wires after all. Maybe we're healthier unhooked from the life-support of consumerism than we imagined. Is there a less-traveled path through our me-first culture that is more adventurous and fulfilling than the one so heavily tread? One that sacrifices none of the good parts of the story, but inspires us to reimagine the sections that are bleeding us all dry?

I think maybe there is.

"It is no accident that despite the fact that bazillions of dollars are spent telling us we are just consumers, and that's all the story we could ever need, people by the thousands and sometimes even millions are frustrated and looking for a better story. And it is here. ... Is it any wonder, if you live your life like a baby bird with your mouth open that what gets dropped into it every time is a worm? People will attempt to reshape your worm and convince you that it is extra yummy this time, but it is still a worm. And the story of consumers is still boring.

"If you are going to get better than that, we're going to have to participate, and go out and seek new sources and resources and options, we're going to have to replace much of our consumption with rituals of non-consumption. We're going to have to write a good and compelling story with our lives. The good news is that it is a lot more fun to be a citizen than a consumer, and rituals of non-consumption are just as satisfying as retail therapy. The good news is that there are better stories out there for the claiming and the living, and events are conspiring to keep our times interesting. The good news is that we can do better than worms."[4, 5]

How did your fast from spending go this week? What did you learn about yourself? What did you notice about your habits? What was difficult? What was surprising? How did God speak in the empty space? Any breakthroughs? Any disappointments? What will you take away?

Week 8

STRESS

Video Notes

Group Guide

How does our culture go against the grain of observing a time for rest?

How is your life right now? Are you running on empty or well-rested in God?

Are there red flags in your schedule or your family's schedule? What can you do to address areas where you're overcommitted?

Video session downloads available at *www.lifeway.com/jenhatmaker*

Getting Ready for Stress

Let me tell you this right up front: You're going to love this week. We're all going to take a breather. No *stop spending money*, no *stop accumulating junk*, no *get off Facebook*, no *quit eating garbage and producing garbage and throwing away garbage that belongs in your recycling bin*. Just … breathe, pray, rest. But first, it's time to settle on your fast this week.

In the original 7 experiment, The Council and I followed the ancients into the practice of prayer pauses every day—described as "breathing spells for the soul."[1] (Doesn't that sound nice?)

Here are the basics so you'll be ready to hit the ground running, if this is the option you choose. Every prayer has a rhythm, a focus, and psalms. See pages 161–163 for a detailed description as you prepare.

1. The Night Watch (midnight): "I am awake through each watch of the night to meditate on Your promise" (Ps. 119:148).
2. The Awakening Hour (dawn): "Satisfy us in the morning with Your faithful love so that we may shout with joy and be glad all our days" (Ps. 90:14).
3. The Blessing Hour (mid-morning): "Let the favor of the Lord our God be on us; establish for us the work of our hands—establish the work of our hands!" (Ps. 90:17)
4. The Hour of Illumination (noon): "You are the salt of the earth. … You are the light of the world" (Matt. 5:13-14).
5. The Wisdom Hour (mid-afternoon): "For me, living is Christ and dying is gain" (Phil. 1:21).
6. The Twilight Hour (twilight): "He got up, rebuked the wind, and said to the sea, 'Silence! Be still!' The wind ceased, and there was a great calm" (Mark 4:39).
7. The Great Silence (bedtime): "The LORD will send His faithful love by day; His song will be with me in the night—a prayer to the God of my life" (Ps. 42:8).

May I offer a tip? Set your phone or watch alarm for your seven pauses. I hit approximately half of each day's prayers the first week until I got wise and set alarms. *You don't have a week to lose*, good friends, so trust me on this: otherwise you'll miss three straight pauses before you even know what happened.

We also observed the Sabbath from sundown on Saturday to sundown on Sunday. In Jewish tradition, Sabbath begins on Friday evening, but we adhered to the spirit of the day (like Jesus so aptly demonstrated with constant abuse of Sabbath's legalistic restrictions but profound devotion to its spirit), which calls for corporate worship and family rest. For us culturally, that day is Sunday.

We prayed as a family when we were together during the pauses. Your kids can read the Scriptures or offer their own sweet prayers. I also invited whoever I was with to join me when the alarm went off (this made for some beautiful moments with my friends). As members of Christ's body, let's pull ourselves off the hamster wheel this week. Prepare your family and your mind.

If you don't tackle seven pauses each day, focus on those you can (remember: alarms help!). Or here are some other options:

- Evaluate your schedule with your family. Make necessary reforms in areas that are overextended, unnecessary, too taxing, or too much. It is OK to say no to good things.
- Identify seven stressors in your life, and evaluate ways to minimize the negative impacts. (Morning routine a mess? Getting up 30 minutes earlier could solve everything. Commute leave you white-knuckled? Download a sermon series or tap into the PG comedy station on Pandora ... my kids are I are obsessed with this.)
- Get up an hour earlier than usual and spend the time reading your Bible or in prayer before God.
- Establish "pause practices" in your family: dinner rituals, breakfast prayers/readings, after-school debriefing, weekend customs. Anything that slows the pace and builds in rest, prayer, and connection.
- Build in a short prayer pause before turning on the TV, pulling up Facebook/Twitter, checking e-mail, making a phone call, starting the car, and turning on music. Prayer might totally revolutionize how we engage our daily environment.

After discussing with your spouse, family, roommates, or partners in crime, how have you decided to fast from stress this week?

What are your concerns?

An Idiot's Guide to Travel

Not too long ago, I was at the Austin airport headed to Atlanta for a conference. I checked in the night before, arrived an hour early, and wore flip-flops to breeze through security, all the things a savvy traveler does. (Related: Despite my superior flying habits, 100 percent of the time I skip the security line with the elderly couple in wheelchairs and instead get behind the sleek business-woman with a briefcase, and inevitably, she is concealing either nunchakus, explosives, or contraband liquor, and the old people are seated on their plane with coffee in hand before I'm through security.)

Anyhow, because my week had included no less than 27 practices, games, events, meetings, gatherings, field trips, conference calls, and deadlines, I arrived to the airport frazzled and depleted. To make matters worse, checking the departure board, I couldn't find my flight to Atlanta anywhere.

White hot panic coursed through my veins, because I'd long worried about this exact moment, the one where I got the date or the time wrong or the confer-ence was *last* weekend or some tragedy. I knew my overwhelmed mind would eventually ruin someone's event, and evidently the moment was upon me.

Flushed and sweaty from panic, I grabbed the first airline employee I could find, shoved my ticket in his hand, and blurted: "I can't find my flight! What happened to my flight? Neither of those flights to Atlanta match my itinerary! I'm freaking out!"

Employee looked at my ticket.

Employee rolled his eyes.

Employee deadpanned: "You're flying to Nashville."

Oh.

You know that thing when you're so overextended and stretched thin and running on fumes, and you simply lose the ability to function like a respon-sible, sane human in even the most familiar, ordinary circumstances and you actually don't even know where you're going?

That.

I know I'm not the only one who runs on empty, good reader. Stress is the calling card of our generation, the proof of our productivity, evidence of our important lives. We're busy. We're incredibly taxed. We're involved in worthwhile and stunning activities. We ensure our kids follow suit, keeping the schedule of a first-year trial lawyer, and the line items sacrificed are family dinners, unplanned afternoons, breathing space, rest.

There is a better way.

Creating room for the Spirit to move us, shift us, redirect us, and center us, God gave us a command that, like fasting, has lost its place as a cornerstone of Christian society.

It started like this: God created the world in six days and on the seventh He rested. "God blessed the seventh day and declared it holy" (Gen. 2:3). First, let's acknowledge that nothing was holy or unholy yet. Nothing was sacred or sanctified. Nothing was evil or sinful. God had blessed other parts of creation, but He'd not consecrated anything as righteous. The animals, seas, mountains, people, plants, stars, sun, birds … all beautiful, all blessed, but none holy.

Read Genesis 2:2–3. According to Scripture, why was the seventh day declared holy by God?

What are the implications of this declaration?

A reader recently wrote a scathing review of 7, loving the first six months but hating the last one, because I "consumed the Sabbath for my own rest and rejuvenation rather than offering it to God." Dear ones, I double-checked this.

Yep. God created the Sabbath so we could rest. It's just that simple.

So sacred was this obedience, it *was* worship, a Sabbath unto God. It established a rhythm essential to healthy community, sustainable agriculture, and equitable society. The Bible is terribly straightforward here. The laying aside of work, the gathering of family and faith community, the self-denial required to be still, the rest; this is holiness. It is for us *from* God and from us *unto* God.

Here is a biblical sound bite. Consider the language carefully:
> "Understand that the LORD has given you the Sabbath" (Ex. 16:29).
> "The seventh day is a Sabbath to the LORD your God. You must not do any work" (Ex. 20:10).
> "On the seventh day there must be a Sabbath of complete rest, dedicated to the LORD" (Ex. 31:15).
> "It is a Sabbath of complete rest for you, and you must practice self-denial" (Lev. 16:31).
> "The seventh day is a Sabbath to the LORD your God. You must not do any work—you, your son or daughter, your male or female slave, your ox or donkey, any of your livestock, or the foreigner who lives within your gates, so that your male and female slaves may rest as you do" (Deut. 5:14).
> "I also gave them My Sabbaths to serve as a sign between Me and them, so they will know that I am Yahweh who sets them apart as holy" (Ezek. 20:12).
> "[Jesus] told them, 'The Sabbath was made for man and not man for the Sabbath'" (Mark 2:27).

How do these verses challenge the notion that the Sabbath is simply one more legalistic rule to keep?

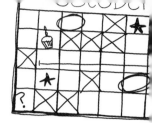

So When is This Thing?

When do we observe Sabbath? There are a zillion discrepancies between the Hebrew calendar and our modern Gregorian one, like the Jewish year beginning in what is our April. Ours is lunar, and the Jewish is lunisolar, having anywhere from 353 to 385 days and 12 months, 13 in a leap year. Our day starts at 12 a.m. The Jewish day begins at sundown. Culturally, the Jewish work week started on Sunday and ran six days. Ours begins Monday and runs five. The Israelites gathered for corporate worship on the seventh day, and we gather on the first.

Just as we don't follow the Jewish calendar in any other way, the heart of Sabbath does not require adherence to ancient calendaring that has no equivalent in the modern civil calendar. Comparing our days and months to theirs is like apples and oranges.

As we must do as children of the Spirit, we ask: What is God's point? What is the intent? When is our day of rest and why? For most of us, it is Sunday. The week recedes and space opens up. Offices and Chick-Fil-A are closed, and churches are opened. "You must keep My Sabbaths and revere My sanctuary" (Lev. 19:30). If that day is Saturday, Wednesday, or Monday for you, please receive the freedom to obey God in your day of rest. As fiercely as God is after our hearts and not perfunctory obedience, we must chase after His.

> "One person considers one day to be above another day. Someone else considers every day to be the same. Each one must be fully convinced in his own mind. Whoever observes the day, observes it for the honor of the Lord." Romans 14:5-6

> "Don't let anyone judge you in regard to food and drink or in the matter of a festival or a new moon or a Sabbath day. These are a shadow of what was to come; the substance is the Messiah." Colossians 2:16-17

By the time of the New Testament letters, we see "church" as we know it in the synagogues every Sabbath.

The two purposes of Sabbath are rest and worship. What competing forces threaten your Sabbath?

Sabbath was introduced in Exodus, when God engaged the Israelites after wandering the desert for a month and a half (only 39 years, 10 and a half months to go, guys!). They'd packed their tents and babies around for an eon, depleted their food, and were kind of over it. Sick and tired of being sick and tired, worn plumb out. They basically said, "We wish we were dead! Or still slaves where we at least got to sit around and eat slabs of meat! We hate everything! Why did you rescue us, Moses, just to watch us starve in this God-forsaken desert?" (I judge this not. If I had to shuttle my family around a hot desert for a month and a half while our food ran out, you'd watch me hyperventilate.)

Read Exodus 16:11-30. Why do you think the Sabbath is wrapped up in the concept of provision (as it was coupled with a food supply)?

We have a wonderful nugget to mine here. Because the Israelites were not yet in charge of their own food supply, God rained down manna for breakfast and quail for dinner every day. Well, almost every day. For six days they received their portion from the skies, but here was the catch: it had to be eaten that day. The manna melted away by noon, and the quail would spoil by the next morning. They both had a super short shelf life.

Because of this food distribution method, God established a portioning system where each family collected exactly what they could eat in one day—no more, no less. Six people? You got six omers. Three people? Here's your three. No point in hoarding extra because unless you gorged that day like a little Miss Piggy, it was all rotten by dawn.

However, on the sixth day, each family gathered twice their regular portion. And miraculously, none of it would spoil by the seventh day, because God established the Sabbath—holy, supernatural, an answer to their prayers—and not only were His people to rest, but He would rest from sending down their food supply. If they didn't gather double portions on the sixth day, they were out o' luck on the seventh, because God was on sabbatical (see what I did there?) and wasn't sending food.

What spiritual insights do you draw from "daily bread: just enough for today" or "trying to live on yesterday's bread" or "no food on the Sabbath unless you gathered it in advance"?

There is never an end to the work, only an end to the week. A Sabbath rest doesn't mean everything is finished. It doesn't signal completed tasks or every mission accomplished. It may find us squarely in the center of a project, neck-deep in unfinished work. It comes every seven days in the middle of life.

Do we not still have to gather double portions the day before? Are there not special preparations to provide for rest? We still have to plan for the Sabbath, tying up loose ends and gathering what we'll need. We still have to prepare our families for rest, enforcing healthy boundaries and protecting our calendar. We still have to set work aside and trust in the wisdom of God's design. "Understand that the LORD has given you the Sabbath" (Ex. 16:29).

What is your history with honoring the Sabbath? Is your day of rest beautiful, worshipful, slow, restful? Or harried, busy, overcommitted, still-working? Or somewhere in between?

Taking cues from Exodus, what would you have to do to "gather a double portion" on Saturday, preparing for rest on Sunday (or whatever day you rest)? What needs to be prepared, decided, omitted, or declared in advance?

Shabbat Shalom!

May I close with a kind nudge (shove) to introduce the Shabbat (Hebrew word for *Sabbath*) dinner this week with your people? In the original 7 experiment, we followed the traditional practice of beginning at dusk the previous evening. So we rolled out Shabbat dinner on Saturday night.

Traditionally, on late Friday afternoon, observant Jews begin Shabbat preparations. The mood is like preparing for the arrival of a special, beloved guest: the house is cleaned, the family dresses up, the best dishes are set, and a festive meal is prepared. Shabbat candles are lit and a blessing recited just before sunset. This ritual, performed by the woman of the house, officially marks the beginning of Shabbat.

The two candles represent two commandments: *zakhor* ("remember" creation and God's deliverance from captivity) and *shamor* ("observe" the day of rest God initiated at creation). The man of the house leads a traditional kiddush, a prayer sanctifying Shabbat while passing a loaf of challah, a sweet bread shaped into a braid. The family then shares a lovely reading together before eating. There are many readings, poems, and Scriptures to use. Google it.

From 7:

> The pizzas smelled up the house like heaven, we set out the "nice" dishes, ... positioned the candles, laid Shabbat readings on each place setting, situated challah bread in the middle, and the family assembled around our lovely table.

A mood accompanies the Sabbath dinner. It is festive and affectionate, expectant and joyful. My littles had happy faces; Sydney asked to do this every week forever. Relief surrounds the evening; the meal is special, the mood is light, and the next 24 hours are wrestled from the grip of stress and frenzy.

Brandon led us through the readings, as I lit two candles representing *remembrance* and *observation*. ... We prayed. We closed with "Shabbat shalom! Shabbat shalom!" Peace on the Sabbath.

Then commenced movie night with popcorn and hot chocolate. The rest of Sabbath involved our beloved church, lunch with friends then home for naps. ...

Delicious food, family, church, friends, rest, worship ... thank You, God. You're smart.[2]

Sabbath is a beautiful practice. Want to give it a try? Anything you need to establish or omit in advance? Anyone God might want you to invite to share it with you, someone who needs some hope and rest?

God gave us a telling glimpse behind the heart of Sabbath when He stretched the concept to include other rest periods:

- The land received a Sabbath, enjoying one year of respite from farming every seven years (see Lev. 25:2-6).
- Farm animals and livestock were extended a Sabbath (see Deut. 5:14).
- Foreigners and non-Hebrew visitors enjoyed the Sabbath (see Deut. 5:14; Isa. 56:3-6).

- Land was returned, debts cancelled, and people redeemed in one of the most overlooked secrets of the Bible: "You are to count seven sabbatical years, seven times seven years, so that the time period of the seven sabbatical years amounts to 49. Then you are to sound a trumpet loudly in the seventh month, on the tenth day of the month; you will sound it throughout your land on the Day of Atonement. You are to consecrate the fiftieth year and proclaim freedom in the land for all its inhabitants. It will be your Jubilee" (Lev. 25:8-10).

Sabbath is a big deal. Very, very big. It is the first thing declared "holy." It involves rest and rhythms and worship and healthy land and freedom and family and faith communities and obedience. It certainly isn't lazy or unproductive. It is still a holy practice, even though the tight restrictions were removed through Jesus, who is "the substance."

It is holy unto God.

We have to breathe. We must. The pace we are keeping isn't sustainable. Who wants it to be? So much is in jeopardy when we refuse obedience here. God connected Sabbath to every inhabitant and animal in His land, and the land itself. The spiritual benefits of Sabbath extend well beyond our small boundaries. We need this. Our families need this. Our faith communities need this.

May we reject the American pace that says *never stop* and instead embrace the exquisite reset button God built into His holy community.

I didn't talk this week about schedules, over-commitment, or unhealthy boundaries. I believe with constant prayer (like the Seven Sacred Pauses facilitate) and weekly Sabbath rest, we will develop the discernment necessary for everything else. The disciplines will slow us down long enough for the Spirit to teach us better practices. Use this space to reflect on the stress in your life and/or your family's life.

What is your response this week?

How has God spoken?

What is easy to embrace? What is challenging?

Pray for guidance and courage. God is for you and with you.

Want more?

- Our kids don't need to do nearly as much as we sign them up for. Make healthy choices for your children, even if that means pulling out of something.
- Consider tithing your time. What would giving away 10 percent of your time look like for you and your family? What would have to do? What would you add?
- Attend a silent prayer retreat (or develop your own).

- The tone of our homes deeply affects stress on the family. Commit to kind, respectful words, and no raised voices for a week. See if a peaceful house is not within reach.
- Develop the habit of rising before the family for prayer and quiet space. This does wonders for the day.
- Maintain the Seven Sacred Pauses beyond this week. They are so lovely and the discipline will absolutely change our lives.

And here are the promised details of the Seven Sacred Pauses:

1. The Night Watch (midnight)

Also called Vigils, *which I love.* "Like Jesus, keeping watch the night before he died, I keep vigil with those who wait alone."[3] This is a deep, even dark prayer of waiting and interceding, keeping vigil with Christ who never sleeps and guards us in our darkest hours (see Isa. 40:28). The Night Watch advocates for others in a dark night of the soul: the suffering, abandoned, oppressed, lonely.

This pause is also powerful silent; a simple, quiet connection with Jesus, staying awake together to shoulder the suffering that plagues this planet and our hearts. "I am at rest in God alone" (Ps. 62:1). There is something powerful about your presence, your attention, the vigil you and Jesus are keeping.

Readings: Psalm 42; Psalm 63; Psalm 119:145-152

2. The Awakening Hour (dawn)

At dawn, it's time to begin our day in glory, remembering God is goodness. Even after the darkest night, the sun will rise. It's the moment to pray for resurrection: Do we need to awaken to joy? Forgiveness? Should we pray for the awakening of love in our hearts for our spouse or children? "Even in darkness light dawns for the upright, for those who are gracious and compassionate and righteous" (Ps. 112:4, NIV).

We enter a new day where our lives can become a living praise. After the Night Watch, this moment celebrates God's intervention, His redemption. We never have to look far to see what He has repaired and whom He has transformed. "This day is Yours, Jesus. Awaken Your love in my heart so that I am a vessel of light today."

Readings: Psalm 19; Psalm 95; Psalm 147

3. The Blessing Hour (mid-morning)

This pause has two emphases: The first is mindfulness of the Spirit's abiding presence. In the middle of the morning, the Holy Spirit came upon the disciples with gifts of courage for birthing a church (Acts 2:15). For this reason, the early church commemorated Terce, or "third hour," a fixed time of prayer in almost all Christian liturgies. At this hour, the opportunities are still endless, making it the perfect time to invite the Spirit. This pause can redirect our morning from "efficient" to "inspired," before the day gets away.

Second, the Blessing Hour is about the sacredness of our work. Whatever our work looks like—an office, raising children, working from home, a classroom, ministry—we ask the Spirit to bless us with creativity, composure, inspiration, love. Visible love is possible if we work mindfully, as carriers of the sweet Spirit of Christ.

Readings: Psalm 67; Psalm 84; Psalm 121

4. The Hour of Illumination (noon)

At midday, we honor the hour Jesus embraced the cross (Matt. 27:45). Like Him, we recommit to giving our lives away. We follow His leadership in servanthood, pledging to shine brightly, becoming hope to the hopeless and light in the darkness.

We ask Jesus to send light into our hearts so they break wide open, and we can make decisions that lead to peace; from death to life, deception to truth, despair to hope, hate to love. We self-inspect our hearts for violence we harbor—toward ourselves, family members, coworkers, community, those who are different. We offer our hands and words as agents of justice. (By all means, enjoy this pause outside with your face turned toward the sun.)

Readings: Psalm 24; Psalm 33; Psalm 34

5. The Wisdom Hour (mid-afternoon)

The Wisdom Hour embraces the themes of surrender, forgiveness, wisdom, and the impermanence of this life. It is the hour Jesus died and gave up His spirit (Mark 15:34). This prayer acknowledges all things are passing; life is temporary and we should live like we believe that.

This hour is the prayer for wisdom to help us live like we we're dying, which we are. Imagine the fearlessness we'd embrace with this understanding. Imagine the risks we would take, the love we would share, the forgiveness we would not withhold, the dreams we would chase. With evening approaching, we pray for *perspective* on this short, fleeting life, and accordingly, we hold out forgiveness, release our grudges, and offer our gifts to the world, understanding we only have a few years to share them.

Readings: Psalm 71; Psalm 90; Psalm 138

6. The Twilight Hour

This is the evening prayer, prayed for centuries at the end of the workday. The main themes are gratitude and serenity as the evening lamps are lit. We invite God's peace as we leave work and transition into dinner, family, home, rest.

A major theme of Vespers is gratitude. No matter the chaos of the day, "If you search out reasons to be grateful, you may be amazed to discover that your gratitude room is overflowing."[4] Even with disorder at this hour, we say, "thank You" for employment, for children and home, for our gifts. We say, "thank You" for hands to labor and love with, and ask for grace for the work of the approaching evening.

Readings: Psalm 34; Psalm 139; Psalm 145

7. The Great Silence (bedtime)

This prayer concludes the day; a beautiful time to pray with children as we tuck them in or with a spouse or friend before we sleep. Also called Compline, from the Latin word for *completion,* it begins with a gentle evaluation of the day. The focus is on awareness, and we include not just weaknesses but the accomplishments of the day. The Great Silence teaches us to be healthy sinners, living in neither denial of our sin, nor despair because of it.

The second theme is darkness—protection from some forms and acceptance of others. We ask the Spirit to guard against our Enemy, protecting our zeal and innocence in Christ. We pray our children are sheltered under God's wings. We confess and repent from the darkness that binds us.

On the other hand, we welcome the soft darkness that is exquisitely beautiful and healing. God dims the lights on our weary bodies, making the way for sleep, allowing us to see the stars.

Readings: Psalm 23; Psalm 91; Psalm 134

Wrap Up

As you process your observations, here are mine. Sigh … I loved this month:

> What a finale to Month Seven! Thanksgiving was epic: we ate our weight in honey ham and fried turkey, jalapeño cranberry relish and my Grandma's carrots, which are legendary and will go down in King Family history. We cooked and laughed and napped and ate again. My mom made pumpkin cheesecake and homemade whipped cream. Clearly nothing can top that, so I'll end this food paragraph on that high note. …
>
> I've discovered I can fast from clothes and waste and spending easier than I can fast from busyness. Wear the same outfit six days straight? Sure. Garden and recycle? No problem. Pause seven times a day in the middle of my life? Now that's asking a lot. I found this month very challenging and equally beautiful. Evidently, I don't respond well to interruptions, Spirit-led or otherwise.
>
> But these pauses, plus the Sabbath, plus the sabbatical taught me something: my heart craves a slower life. I want people to stop prefacing their phone calls with this: "I know you're so busy, but if I could just have a second …" I want to figure out what this means for our family. We can't live in the barn forever, nor we can pull out of work, ministry, school, community, mission, family, and all the activities that accompany them. But what can we do to cultivate a quiet, ranch heart in a noisy, urban world?
>
> I know we'll be keeping the Sabbath. Um, hold your applause since we've been instructed to do this from Exodus to Hebrews. As God explained at the inauguration of the Sabbath:
>
> "Remember the Sabbath day by keeping it holy. Six days you shall labor and do all your work, but the seventh day is a sabbath to the LORD your God. On it you shall not do any work, neither you, nor your son or daughter, nor your male or female servant, nor your animals, nor any foreigner residing in your towns. For in six days the LORD made the heavens and the earth, the sea, and all that is in them, but he rested on the seventh day. Therefore the LORD blessed the Sabbath day and made it holy" (Ex. 20:8-11, NIV).

Is it coincidental that God named every person included in the rest? Sons and daughters, servants and animals, guests and visitors; we all need this. My neglect of the Sabbath doesn't just affect me but my entire household, my extended community. The pace we keep has jeopardized our health and happiness, our worship and rhythms. We belong to a culture that can't catch its breath; rather, we refuse to catch our breath.

God doesn't pull any punches here: The Sabbath is holy. Not lazy, not selfish, not unproductive; not helpful, not optional, not just a good idea. *Holy*. Like God demonstrated in Exodus 16, He'll provide for daily needs, but on the sixth day, He'll rain down a double portion to store up for the Sabbath, covering our needs while we rest. The only day a double collection wouldn't spoil by dawn's light was the Sabbath; God made a way. ...

My heart feels renewed at the completion of the month. Perhaps the greatest gift is clarity. My mission is concentrated: this matters, this doesn't, this counts, this doesn't. It's actually not that complicated. The Bible is true, no matter how contrary to reality it appears. I've discovered you can press extremely hard on the Word, and it will hold.

It is healing to forgive.

You *do* gain your life by losing it.

Love *does* truly conquer evil.

A simple life really is liberating.[5]

How did your fast from stress go this week? What did you learn about yourself? What did you notice about your habits? What was difficult? What was surprising? How did God speak in the empty space? Any breakthroughs? Any disappointments? What will you take away?

Week 9

WRAP UP

Video Notes

Group Guide

Which week of The 7 Experiment was the most difficult for you? Which was the easiest? Why?

How has removing excess made you more aware of God's kingdom work?

What have you learned about yourself and your heart?

What has most changed you? Where do you still need to work?

Even though a fast isn't permanent, are there any behavior changes you've made or want to make permanent? Why these specific changes?

Video session downloads available at www.lifeway.com/jenhatmaker

Conclusions and Takeaways

During my original 7 experiment, my friends and I ran in the Chosen Marathon for Adoption, raising money to bring Ben and Remy home. I gathered sponsors for each mile, posting blogs, updates, and pictures designed to ~~guilt~~ inspire folks to kick in to our adoption kitty. We bought good shoes, fancy socks, and packets of energy goo that should be used as punishment for serial killers. We researched chafing tips, carb-loading schedules, hydration practices, and heart rate monitors. We scattered our business on Facebook and Twitter.

The only thing we left out was training.

I mean, we "sort of trained" (finger quotes are necessary here), meaning we took long walks sometimes. Oh sure, we'd say, "run to the next light post" and "run to the end of the street," but we preferred walking. As I said to my friends once: "Let's just walk so we can talk more. I can't breathe with all this running."

One time, *once,* we ran/walked 7 miles. It's the farthest we ever went, figuring if we could run/walk 7, we could knock out 13.1. What's the difference? Anything over half a mile is ludicrous and all the same. (I have a hate/hate relationship with running.)

On race day, we hit the halfway mark with ease. Spirits were high. No goo was consumed yet. Muscles and feet were cooperating. We'd passed our church's water station at top speed of course, as if they would see us doing anything but practically sprinting. Sure, the lead half-marathoner passed us on his return about mile 4, but these people were like genetically modified robots. They had no business running with a bunch of adopters more interested in the spaghetti the night before than injury prevention.

But slightly after the halfway mark, things took a turn for the worse. Something appeared to be wrong with my legs. My hips sent my brain a message that said: "Listen here, you think you can trot us out to do the dirty work after totally neglecting us the last three months? Well think again, missy! MUTINY!" My calves, shins, heels, lungs … they were all in on the revolt.

I started bargaining with God, not so much for endurance but for the Rapture to end this nonsense. Euphoria and pharmaceuticals propelled us over the finish line and eased us through the next two days of paralysis and blisters. But I learned something: The training part slightly affected the race part. Train well, run well. Train poorly, run poorly.

This is the best metaphor to explain what 7 was to me: training. It wasn't even the race. It definitely wasn't the finish line. It was simply the very, very necessary work required in advance if I have any hope of running a good race. It was trimming down and culling the excess, developing new muscles and habits. It involved disciplined obedience to run leaner, faster, stronger. Fasting throughout 7 was preparation; the Big Race is coming.

I cannot run the race weighed down with so much excess; the indulgences sabotage the pace. All this time I've been slogging through the kingdom, dragging my luxuries and entitlement behind me. I've tried so hard to carry them. I've shoved and folded and packed and roped them in, unwilling to leave them behind, attempting to still run.

But as I slowly (and sometimes begrudgingly) dropped a few extravagances on the shoulder, something happened: not only did the pace pick up, but I suddenly noticed other weary, hungry, beautiful people littered along the course, sidelined by hunger and disease and poverty. I hadn't really seen them before, too preoccupied with maintaining my bulky pack. When my hands were emptied of carrying my own entitlement, I was free to slip my arm around their waists, walking those first tentative steps with them until they got their legs under them.

I'm not the only runner in this human race. This is not simply about my personal time. Because we live in a broken, sinful, depleted world, we who are strong are required to bear with those who are weak. This is standard Race Policy. We signed on for that at registration. The runners with water and strength and reserves are to carry those who have none left. If we are racing lean and strong, God can use us to bolster the weary traveler and help him across the finish line.

After eight weeks of 7, where do you feel you are in the race metaphor? Still slogging through training? Loosening up? Ready to run? Talk about your progress.

Abundance and Its Tricky Lies

A great task and vision is set before the church, and it will require complete upheaval for most of us, because our Western perspective is simply too skewed toward our own advantages. We don't even know how else to think. The church hasn't led us much better, guilty of adopting a similar prosperity outlook and sprinkling Jesus on top.

For whom is the abundant life? Those of us lucky enough to be born in America? And does it include such egregious luxuries that literally displace entire nations from the global table? How can God's people sit on so much wealth while the rest of the world gasps for breath and claws for life?

Jesus said in John 10:10:

"A thief comes only to steal and to kill and to destroy. I have come so that they may have life and have it in abundance."

How has material abundance stolen, killed, and destroyed spiritual abundance in our lives?

Often during 7, I felt very, very small, utterly inadequate for the reforms required, the tasks ahead. I still do. This is no sage's manifesto but a sinner's repentance, I assure you. The Enemy whispers lies to me constantly:

"It doesn't really matter."

This is the first one. *God doesn't care about your lifestyle, Jen. He's pleased with decades of theological pontificating and feeding the fattened sheep. That's good. That's enough. Plus, your financial and ecological spending doesn't really affect anyone. None of that is connected to global inequality. You're making way too big of a deal out of excess. This is a small line item spiritually. Lighten up! The earth is fine. It will regenerate endlessly. Use as much as you want and stop telling people this matters. Personal holiness and morality is really the stuff of Christianity. Take your cues from mainstream evangelicalism, not the cries of the oppressed.*

Do you hear this lie too? How does the Enemy tell you that none of this excess really matters?

"None of these changes will really matter."

This is the second one. *Who cares if you recycle your cereal boxes and use less gas? Like it will even make a difference! So what if you tap into a local food supply instead of processed food at the big stores? It won't change farming practices or national health or even your own kids; you know they'll buy boxes of donuts and sodas the second they move out. No one else cares. The church doesn't even care. You're on your own and you're way too insignificant to make a lick of difference. Just do what you want. Extreme poverty will always exist and the orphan crisis will only get worse and people will continue to starve every single day no matter what you do or don't do. Why try?*

How does the Enemy tell you none of these changes will matter?

"Your hypocrisies disqualify you from this entire conversation."

This is the third one, and the lie that burrows the deepest. *You going to tell your Facebook friends that you just bought a new shirt? Yeah, better keep that a secret, hypocrite. How dare you raise these difficult subjects when you still waste, spend, stress, neglect, consume, and hoard. You're guilty times seven. If people knew the areas you still struggle and blatantly disobey, you'd be laughed out of town. Sideline yourself, liar. Until you are a model of responsible spending and lean living and radical generosity and fearless obedience, you stay out of this conversation. Your small changes and reforms are insignificant. They don't count. This is an all-or-nothing deal, and you're not an "all" so you're a "nothing."*

How does the Enemy try to disqualify you?

Coming Back to Life

Allow me to close our time together with truth, because the Enemy uses a whole bag of lies to keep us safely distanced from this discussion, whether through justification, apathy, or shame. None of these messages would ever come from Jesus, who doesn't use these tactics with His beloved sons and daughters. Romans 8 has all we need.

Read Romans 8:1-4. (Theology much?) Paul definitely acknowledged the problem. What are all the downsides of "the flesh"? List everything Paul said.

According to verse 4, what has Jesus accomplished for us?

These are two different realities that coexist, but not for believers. We are well acquainted with the limits of the flesh. We know how we struggle. We know we're a hot mess. We know we can say one thing and do the opposite. It's no surprise to us that sin and death have sunk their filthy claws deeply in our hearts, weakening the law and rendering it powerless. We know that on our own, unchecked, the final chapter of our life stories will read: *condemned*.

The problem with persisting in this paradigm is that it's just not true for believers anymore. It was true, but Jesus completely changed the story, and now there is absolutely no condemnation left for us. He didn't prop us up. He didn't whitewash our errors or look the other way or just give us a new set of rules to try harder. That wouldn't be just, and God cannot act unjustly. The consequences of our sin had to fall somewhere.

Jesus took all our shame. All of it. There is none left. You cannot attach condemnation to your life if you are a Christ-follower anymore. You just can't. There isn't any left to give you. This has nothing to do with you, outside of your faith in Jesus. This is God's grace to us through Jesus' sacrifice, nothing more. This is salvation; we are saved from ourselves, saved from shame, saved from guilt. The requirements of the law are fully met in us. It doesn't mean we act perfect now, but Jesus is perfect for us, in us. Our sin no longer requires salvation, only sanctification. We were once *guilty*, but now we are simply *convicted*, because we are children of the Spirit; His saving power trumps our shame and sin. Sorry if you'd rather hang onto those ballasts, but they are obsolete.

Shame has no place in this 7 discussion. What do you need to release to receive freedom through Jesus?

Read Romans 8:12-17. What competing messages do we receive from a "spirit of fear" and the "Spirit of adoption" as it relates to excessive consumption? Have you been listening to one more than the other? Talk about that.

According to Paul, we are no longer obligated to that old sinful nature. I adore this statement so much. We're free. We don't have to follow any old rules just because they are familiar or comfortable. We don't have to chase notoriety or wealth or security anymore, the dance cards of society. Our future is secure, so we are liberated to live a subversive, countercultural life following none of the typical rules, no matter who thinks we've lost our ever-loving minds. (I know the last couple of years have made me feel a teeny bit crazy.)

Without Jesus, what alternative would we have? Those old rules elevate creature comforts, self-advancement strategies; the tools of the self-made man. The law of sin and death says, "Protect yourself, for you are on your own." And without Jesus we are. But the law of the Spirit says, "You are safely Mine, so you can trust Me with everything you have, everything you own, everything you earn because your spirit is *alive now.*"

Being alive is so much better than being dead.

In terms of reducing, what old rules of self-preservation (sin and death) are hard to let go of? What makes you feel "radical" or "crazy" or "petrified"?

I've heard the whispers of life throughout 7. I've felt my heart crackle and flash to life, confirming that yes, this, *this is living.* This is the stuff of beauty and true abundance and kingdom. I was forfeiting my soul to gain the world, but Jesus is winning it back. I'm learning. I'm starting to believe it.

Suffering, Labor, Redemption, and Hope

Paul said we are adopted children, heirs of God and coheirs with our Jesus (if that is not the most mind-boggling phrase ever), "if indeed we share in his sufferings" (Rom. 8:17, NIV). When we were stuck in the Ethiopian court system for our son, staring down an impending rejection for his adoption, we hit darkness. Month after month stretched out, as our children waited for us, victims of a difficult, chaotic system. A black cloud hovered over me and I could not shake it. *It would not be shook, I tell you.*

During that time, well-meaning friends offered many versions of this statement: "Chin up! Find joy in this! This is all God's timing, so don't worry!" Good reader, I know this came from loving hearts, but it would not pierce my grief. My spirit would not receive this, no matter how much I prayed and faked it.

Finally I screamed in desperation: "I *am* worried, God! I *am* devastated! My children are on another continent wondering why we haven't come back for them, and they are going to bed without a mom and dad tonight *again,* and my heart is broken! I will *not* put my chin up! I will *not* skip around like Pollyanna! I am angry and sad and hurting for them and raging against the political systems that keep children in orphanages and families in poverty! If grieving for them is wrong, I do not want to be right ever again in my life!"

Very quietly, very clearly, God spoke to me: "When I asked you to adopt, I invited you into the suffering of the orphan. That suffering includes all their losses, all their grief, all their fear. You are suffering with them right now, because that is part of the deal. You will suffer with them even more once they get home. When you said yes to adoption, you agreed to enter their brokenness and live there with them until they were healed. Obeying Me means suffering with those who suffer, which is dark and painful and it *hurts.* You don't get to live a happy, oblivious life while My vulnerable ones grieve. Jesus was a Man of sorrows, acquainted with grief, and you are His disciple. You are not wrong … *you are following Me into the kingdom.*"

"If indeed we share in his sufferings in order that we may also share in his glory." Romans 8:17, NIV

We are no longer obligated to sin nature, but we are obligated to share in Jesus' suffering. For whom did He suffer? Who broke His heart? Who moved Him to action and mercy?

What sort of suffering does the church sign up for when we act justly and love mercy? In what places and with whom would you expect to find people obedient to this mandate?

Read Romans 8:18-25. How do you relate to the frustration and futility described in this passage? Do broken people and broken creation just totally overwhelm you sometimes? Talk about living in a world with so much suffering.

Like Paul observed, this feeling of endless labor is not just around us but within us. We feel it too, don't we? The earth is filled with groaning and waiting and frustration and bondage and decay. One need not look far to find it. Mamas are burying their babies and the sick are dying alone. Hunger steals life in a world with enough food to feed us all. Humans are sold as property; innocence is ruined. Creation itself longs for liberation, anxious to be set free from the effects of human sin. We are all hungry for deliverance.

But there is also much good news in this passage, for Paul speaks of glory and eager expectation and freedom and redemption and hope. No labor, however long, lasts forever. We know Jesus will make all things new. We know our hope is well placed. We know tears will be dried and suffering will end. We know God will make the last first and the least the greatest. The meek will indeed inherit the earth. Glory is coming.

Read Romans 8:26-30. If the Spirit intercedes for us "according to the will of God," what elements of His will do you see in verses 28-30?

What connection do you see between verses 28-30 and verse 19?

I'll end this study the same way I started it: with a question from Ben. Just this morning, as he and I were the only two awake in the house, he asked me:

"Mom? Is life fair?"

I paused, because he has endured such heartache. His eight years have been spectacularly unfair, and I so wanted to assure him that here, here with us forever, life is safe and permanent and so very fair. But none of those descriptors are true, and my kid wasn't born yesterday. A hard life wizened him up far sooner than it should have. So I told him: "No. Life isn't fair. It's so not fair. It wasn't fair that you and Remy ended up in an orphanage as little kids. It wasn't fair that so many parents in your country died or couldn't raise their children. It isn't fair that we have everything we've ever needed and you went hungry. I wish the world was fair, but it isn't."

My sharp son asked, "But God is big enough. Why doesn't He just make everything fair?"

I told him the same thing I'll tell you: God raised up one man, then through him one family, then through them an entire nation, His special treasure to tell His story to the world. But one nation wasn't enough; God sent Jesus to redeem all of us, "that He would be the firstborn among many brothers" (Rom. 8:29). Salvation spread to all nations; mankind entered grace in Jesus.

And because the earth is suffering, God said: Here is what I'll do. I'll give My sons and daughters the Word. In it, I'll tell them everything I love. I'll urge them to act justly, to love mercy, and to walk humbly with Me. I'll tell them to care for orphans and widows and prisoners and sick people. I'll make sure they know that love is always first; love Me, love others … everything else hinges on these. I'll send them to the poor, the outcast, the lost and lonely. My people will be hope-bearers. My church will welcome the forgotten, intercede for the forsaken. My Spirit will conform them into the image of Jesus, who rescued the whole earth. Life is not fair … but My people will bring justice in My name.

They will make it fairer.

We are called, justified, glorified. We are changing into the likeness of Jesus, our Brother. We have been called according to God's purpose. While we live and breathe, we will make the earth fairer or die trying. We will call unjust systems to reform and defend the cause of the fatherless. We will question an economic system where 20 percent of earth's inhabitants consume 86 percent of its resources. We will refuse complicity in the ravaging of creation. We will demand justice for the innocent and abused. We will live simply so others can simply live. We will acknowledge the inequity that we perpetuate and repent, offering our lives to Jesus for His cause.

We will be brave.

We will be strong in Jesus.

We will become agents of justice and love and reckless mercy.

We will do this in God's name and for His glory.

We will not be afraid, because "if God is for us, who can be against us?" (Rom. 8:31). After all, "He who did not spare his own Son, but gave him up for us all" (v. 32, NIV) is the One asking us to give until it hurts, share until we break, cross the finish line gasping for air, having poured every last drop out until there is absolutely nothing left.

So that on our last day, we can offer Him our bodies—used, consumed, worn fully out for the kingdom—and He will transform them into glory. And with us will stand the ones He sent us to, the vulnerable He aimed to rescue through the love of His people; the ones we refused to ignore. And together, we will join hands and praise the King of kings, redeemed, restored, children of glory.

"Christ Jesus is the One who died, but even more, has been raised;

He also is at the right hand of God and intercedes for us.

Who can separate us from the love of Christ?

Can *affliction*

or *anguish*

or *persecution*

or *famine*

or *nakedness*

or *danger*

or *sword?*

As it is written: Because of You we are being put to death all day

long; we are counted as sheep to be slaughtered. No, in all these

things *we are more than victorious through Him who loved us.*

For I am persuaded that

not even *death* or *life*,

angels or *rulers*,

things present

or *things to come,*

hostile powers,

height or *depth,*

or *any other created thing*

will have the power to separate us from the love of God

that is in Christ Jesus our Lord!"

Romans 8:34-39

Final Wrap Up

As you process final takeaways from 7 (although they won't be the last, as I sit here two years after the initial experiment, bawling my eyes out), let me share with you an excerpt from my original final conclusion:

> How do I summarize 7, an experiment that has forever altered our lives? My takeaways are so vast, I can't keep an idea still long enough to write about it. New thoughts have so usurped old thoughts, I can't remember what I used to think about. I've ingested information through a fire hose and find myself sputtering and gasping. However, after curbing my appetites for so long, I've discovered my appetites have changed.
>
> I realize some of you are hoping for a romantic ending here, something with aplomb, a juicy Twitter sound bite ("Jen Hatmaker moved from the suburbs to a van down by the river with her five kids. Astonishing. #Seven #readit"). You're waiting for some surprise radical ending I've been saving to drop on my readers, like becoming missionaries or farmers or the quirky stars of a new *Simple Life* segment on *The Today Show* ("Welcome back, Hatmakers!" "Thanks, Matt! Good to be here again!" "Wow! Great dress, Jen!" "Thank you. I sewed it out of discarded plastic bags dredged up from the bottom of polluted lakes." "You are truly amazing." "It's all for Jesus, Matt.")
>
> But that's not where we are. Honestly, we're not sure what's next for the Hatmakers. We know something new is coming; we recognize the winds of change that seem to blow on our little life with regularity. *Seven* allowed us to slowly break up with some of our ideas, our luxuries. It was something of a long good-bye. It's not you, it's us. Well, it *is* you.
>
> However, even if I had a clear directive, I'm not sure I'd share it here. Whatever God has done or is doing in our family is certainly not a template, and I don't want it to be. We live in a certain city with a certain task, we have specific gifts and we're horribly deficient in others. Our life looks like it does because we are the Hatmakers, and God is dealing with us the way He's dealing with us. We have history and sin issues and circumstances and geography that God takes into account as He stakes our place in His kingdom.

You have an entirely different set of factors. I have no idea what this might look like in your life, nor do I want that job. Your story is God's to write, not mine. Some of us are going to live in the suburbs, others downtown. I'm going to garden, you're going to take the subway. We're adopting, you're redistributing, they're downsizing. I use words, you use a hammer. There isn't a list here. There is no stencil we can all trace into our lives in perfect unison. Here is our baseline as a faith community:

Love God most. Love your neighbor as yourself. This is everything.

If we say we love God, then we will care about the poor.

This earth is God's and everything in it. We should live like we believe this.

What we treasure reveals what we love.

Money and stuff have the power to ruin us.

Act justly, love mercy, walk humbly with God. This is what is required.

Steven, our [community garden] partner, asked me this morning while harvesting carrots and potatoes and lettuce: "Who is your reader?" and that got me thinking about you. I'm going to guess you are probably a middle- to upper-middle class parent (but love to my nonbreeders!), and mostly, your life is terribly blessed. Your world is pretty controlled: kids are in good schools, neighborhood is safe, jobs are fairly secure, wardrobe is impressive enough. These advantages cause you some tension, but you're not sure why or what to do with it.

You're likely a believer, but whether you're a lifer or a recent devotee, I'm not sure. A few of you are teetering on the edge of faith, drawn in by Jesus but repelled by His followers. As for church, you probably go to one, but a bunch of you don't; the elitism and waste and bureaucracy became too much and you left, or you want to leave. Some of you are solid attenders, but you feel like crawling out of your skin sometimes, valuing faith community but worried yours is missing the point. A few of you have found the church of your dreams. Half of you read *Radical*, or *Crazy Love*, ... and since you're reading this, you might've read *Interrupted*. You loved and hated it.

I'm guessing you've cried over orphans or refugees or starvation or child prostitutes, heartbroken by the depravity of this world. It's not OK that your kids get school and birthday parties while Third World children get abandoned and trafficked, but you don't know how to fix that. You're wondering if your lifestyle is connected to these discrepancies, and you have a nagging suspicion that less is more but it's a muddy concept. Everyone has ideas. It's confusing and overwhelming. This creates a sort of war within, and it leaves you raw. Sometimes, you're a full-blown mess over it.

Hear this: I don't think God wants you at war with yourself.

He sent the Prince of Peace to soothe those tumultuous waters already. Self-deprecation is a cruel response to Jesus, who died and made us righteous. Guilt is not Jesus' medium. He is battling for global redemption right now; His objective hardly includes huddling in the corner with us, rehashing our shame again. He finished that discussion on the cross. Plus, there's no time for that.

We're so conditioned to being a problem, that we've forgotten we're actually the answer. God is not angry at you; how could He possibly be? You are His daughter, His son, you're on the team. Don't imagine He is sitting us all down for a lecture. Rather, He's staging a rally, gathering the troops. The church is rising like a phoenix right now, collecting speed and strength and power.

Something marvelous and powerful is happening in the church. The Bride is awakening and the Spirit is rushing. It is everywhere. This movement is not contained within a denomination or demographic, not limited to a region or country. It's sweeping up mothers and pastors and teenagers and whole congregations. A stream became a current, and it is turning into a raging flood. It is daily gathering conspirators and defectors from the American Dream. It is cresting with the language of the gospel: the weak made strong, the poor made rich, the proud made humble.

The body of Christ is mobilizing in unprecedented numbers. Jesus is staging a massive movement to bind up the brokenhearted and proclaim freedom for captives. The trumpet is blowing. We are on the cusp, on the side of the Hero. So while we're mistakenly warring with ourselves, Jesus is waging war on injustice and calling us to join Him.

This is way more fun than self-condemnation, no?

So imagine me linking arms with you, giving you an affectionate Texas squeeze. Guilt might be the first chapter, but it makes for a terrible story. Jesus gave us lots of superior material to work with. If your stuff and spending and waste and stress are causing you tension like mine is, just do the next right thing. Ask some new questions; conversation partners are everywhere (their name is Legion, for they are many). Take a little baby step. Tomorrow, you can take another. Offer yourself the same grace Jesus has given you. We're no good to Him stuck in paralysis.

I value you desperately, my sisters and brothers in this adventure. I marvel at your gifts; you're so essential to this conversation. I am stunned by the collective goodness of the Bride. As I hear stories of intervention and reduction and courage, I applaud Jesus in selecting you for your tasks. We serve an unruly Savior on a recklessly wild ride; I'm glad you're on it with me. May we embrace unity over infighting, bravery over comfort, *us* over *me*, people over principles, and God's glory over our own. Together, let's become repairers of broken walls and restorers of streets with dwellings.

"The LORD bless you and keep you; the LORD make his face shine on you and be gracious to you; the LORD turn his face toward you and give you peace" (Num. 6:24-26, NIV).[1]

How has God moved in you during the past nine weeks of The 7 Experiment? What did you learn while fasting from areas of excess? What was the biggest or hardest challenge? What is the next right thing for you to do? How has God changed you?

Wrap Up

Endnotes

Week 1

1. Global Rich List [online, cited 15 July 2012]. Available on the Internet: *www.globalrichlist.com*.
2. "2009 World Population Data Sheet," *Population Reference Bureau* [online], 2009 [cited 5 August 2012]. Available from the Internet: *www.PRB.org*.
3. "The Twelve Steps and the Twelve Traditions," *Alcoholics Anonymous* [online, cited 5 August 2012]. Available from the Internet: *www.aa.org*.
4. Bill Bright, "Your Personal Guide to Fasting and Prayer," *Campus Crusade for Christ* [online, cited 5 Aug. 2012]. Available from the Internet: *www.billbright.com/howtofast*.

Week 2

1. *Self Nutrition Data* [online, cited 5 August 2012]. Available from the Internet: *www.nutritiondata.self.com*.
2. Michael Pollan, *In Defense of Food: An Eater's Manifesto* (New York: Penguin Books, 2008), 13–14.
3. Ibid., 6–7.
4. "Leading Causes of Death," *Centers for Disease Control and Prevention* [online, cited 5 August 2012]. Available from the Internet: *www.cdc.gov*.
5. Pollan, *In Defense of Food*, 10.
6. "Explosion of child obesity predicted to shorten US life expectancy," *EurekAlert!* [online], 16 March 2005 [cited 5 August 2012]. Available from the Internet: *www.eurekalert.org*.
7. "Food, Inc. Film Description," *PBS* [online, cited 5 Aug. 2012]. Available from the Internet: *www.pbs.org/pov/foodinc/film_description.php*.
8. *Halley's Bible Handbook*, 24th ed. (Grand Rapids, MI: Zondervan Publishing House, 1965), 138.
9. Jen Hatmaker, *Seven: An Experimental Mutiny Against Excess* (Nashville: B&H Publishing Group, 2012), 42–43.

Week 3

1. Benjamin R. Barber, *Consumed: How Markets Corrupt Children, Infantilize Adults, and Swallow Citizens Whole* (New York: WW Norton and Company, Inc., 2007), 9.
2. Ibid., 10–11.
3. Hatmaker, *Seven*, 66–68.

Week 4

1. Randy Alcorn, *The Treasure Principle* (Sisters, OR: Multnomah Publishers Inc., 2001), 8.
2. Richard Rohr, *Simplicity: The Freedom of Letting Go* (New York: The Crossroad Publishing Company, 2003)58.
3. Ibid., 59–60.
4. Hatmaker, *Seven*, 92–94.

Week 5

1. Robert Kubey, "2003: Why U.S. media education lags behind the rest of the English-speaking world," *Television and new media*, vol. 4 (4), Nov. 2003, 357.
2. Matt Richtel, "Attached to technology and paying a price," *NY Times* [online], 6 June 2012 [cited 5 Aug. 2012]. Available from the Internet: *www.nytimes.com*.
3. Ibid.
4. Hatmaker, *Seven*, 115–116.

Week 6

1. Wendell Berry, *What Are People For?* (New York: North Point Press, 1990), 98.
2. Steven Bouma-Prediger, *For the Beauty of the Earth: A Christian Vision for Creation Care* (Grand Rapids, MI: Baker Academic, 2010), 20.
3. Kerry Zobor, "Living Planet Report details dangers of living beyond the environment's means," *World Wildlife Fund* [online], 29 Oct. 2008 [cited 5 Aug. 2012]. Available from the Internet: *www.worldwildlife.org*.
4. "Reckless consumption depleting earth's natural resources," *Red Orbit* [online], 29 October 2008 [cited 5 Aug. 2012]. Available from the Internet: *www.redorbit.com*.
5. Rosemary Ruether, "The Biblical Vision of the Ecological Crisis," *Religion Online* [online, cited 5 August 2012]. Available from the Internet: *www.religion-online.org*.
6. Ibid.
7. Tracey Bianchi, *Green Mama* (Grand Rapids, MI: Zondervan, 2010), 18–19.
8. Ruether, "The Biblical Vision."
9. "Steps to Stop Junk Mail," *NYU Law* [online, cited 5 August 2012]. Available on the Internet: *www.law.nyu.edu*.
10. Bouma-Prediger, *For the Beauty of the Earth*, 182.
11. Hatmaker, *Seven*, 148–150.

Wrap Up

Week 7

1. "The State of Human Development," *Human Development Reports* [online] 1998, [cited 5 Aug. 2012]. Available from the Internet: *hdr.undp.org*.
2. "Changing Today's Consumption Patterns—for Tomorrow's Human Development," *Human Development Reports* [online], 1998 [cited 5 August 2012]. Available from the Internet: *hdr.undp.org*.
3. Barber, *Consumed*, 292.
4. Sharon Astyk, "Why I Hate Earth Day," *Science Blogs* [online], 21 April 2010 [cited 5 August 2012]. Available from the Internet: *http://scienceblogs.com*.
5. Hatmaker, *Seven*, 175–177.

Week 8

1. Macrina Wiederkehr, *Seven Sacred Pauses* (Notre Dame, IN: Sorin Books, 2008), 6.
2. Hatmaker, *Seven*, 197–198.
3. Wiederkehr, *Seven Sacred Pauses*, 29.
4. Ibid., 138.
5. Hatmaker, *Seven*, 213–215.

Week 9

1. Hatmaker, *Seven*, 217–221.